OUT of
HIDING

OTHER TITLES YOU MIGHT BE INTERESTED IN:

*Destined to Live: A True Story of
a Child in the Holocaust*
by Ruth Gruener

My Survival: A Girl on Schindler's List
by Rena Finder with Joshua M. Greene

*Hidden Like Anne Frank:
14 True Stories of Survival*
by Marcel Prins and Peter Henk Steenhuis

Survivors: True Stories of Children in the Holocaust
by Allan Zullo and Mara Bovsun

Prisoner B-3087
by Alan Gratz, a novel based on the true story
by Ruth and Jack Gruener

OUT of HIDING

A Holocaust Survivor's
Journey to America

RUTH GRUENER
with Rachel Klein

Scholastic Press / New York

Library of Congress Cataloging-in-Publication Data available

ISBN 978-1-338-62745-9

10 9 8 7 6 5   23 24

Printed in the U.S.A.   37

First edition, October 2020

Book design by Keirsten Geise

To my children and grandchildren

FOREWORD

Imagine that to save your life, you had to sleep curled up inside a trunk for twelve hours a day.

Or spend hour after hour—for years—sitting perfectly still in a corner, never speaking, never moving a muscle, for fear that someone would hear you or see you and send you to your death.

Imagine staying hidden away for so long you forget what trees look like. What the sky looks like. You even forget how to walk.

Imagine being in so much danger that you would

plan your own execution to save the lives of the people hiding you away.

All that—and more—happened to Ruth Gruener when she was a child in the Holocaust.

I first met Ruth when I was asked to help her husband, Jack Gruener, write the story of *his* life as a boy during the Holocaust. When I began to work on Jack's book, my family and I flew to New York City to meet Jack and Ruth. They were two of the kindest people I ever met. We spent the morning at the Museum of Jewish Heritage, where Ruth worked as a docent and had donated some artifacts (a pair of socks she wore from her time in hiding during the war). Then we went back to Jack and Ruth's home. There, while I interviewed Jack for the book I was writing, he and Ruth plied me and my family with more food than ten families could eat—in defiance, perhaps, of the years they had both spent starving during the Holocaust.

The book I wrote with Jack, *Prisoner B-3087*, tells the story of how he survived ten different concentration camps during World War II. Toward the end of Jack's book, he meets a young woman named Luncia—who changes her name to Ruth when she moves to the United States, and eventually becomes Jack's wife.

Jack shows up halfway through this book, *Out of Hiding*. So for all the readers who write to me begging to find out what happens to Jack once his book ends, now you'll know!

Ruth's story echoes another novel I wrote called *Refugee*. That book is not about Ruth *or* Jack—at least not specifically. But like the characters in *Refugee*, Ruth is driven from her home, and with her family must cross stormy seas on their journey to another country, where they will have to learn a new language and a new way of life to survive. Ruth and her family, like millions of others before them and since around the world, were refugees.

Roughly 250,000 European Jews were displaced by World War II, and many of those refugees, like Ruth and her family, hoped to immigrate to America after the war. But the application process wasn't easy. The American government kept changing the rules, sometimes from day to day. Ruth and her family persisted, though, and were lucky to eventually end up in the United States. And the United States was lucky to have them.

As I remind students when I tell them about Jack's story, unfortunately, the last generation of Holocaust survivors is passing away. That's why it's more important than ever that we hear their stories directly from them, while we still can. Ruth Gruener understands this. I hear her voice loud and clear in every sentence of this book, as though Ruth is right here in the room telling me everything that happened to her. Now her story will live on for generations in her own words.

Silence is dangerous, Ruth tells us. If you don't tell your own story, someone else will tell it for you—and maybe not the way you'd like it to be told. This book, and the decades Ruth has spent telling people her story in schools and gathering places around the world, is a testament to the power of speaking up, speaking out, and speaking your own truth.

Alan Gratz
Asheville, NC
2019

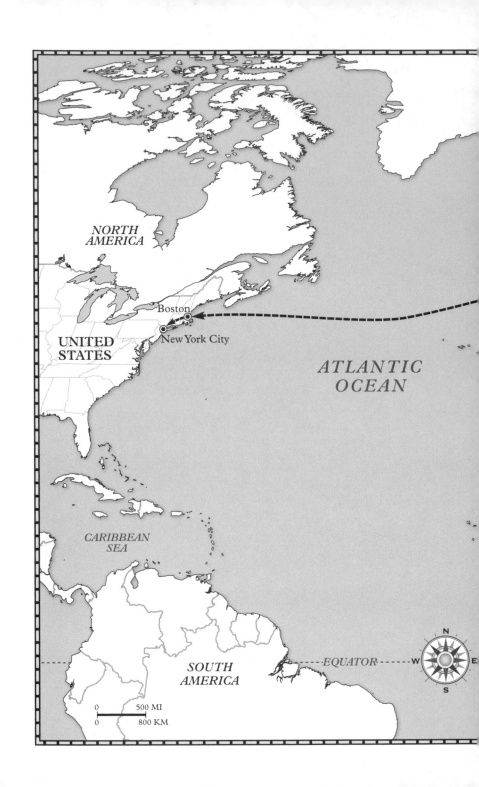

AREA OF DETAIL

NORTH
SEA

Hamburg

E U R O P E

BLACK SEA

NORTH
SEA

BALTIC
SEA

Hamburg
Bremen
GERMANY

POLAND

Kraków

Lvov

UKRAINE

Munich
Steyr
AUSTRIA

E U R O P E

BLACK SEA

MEDITERRANEAN
SEA

0   200 MI
0   300 KM

Prologue: Remembering

IT WAS A LATE morning in the spring of 2018, and I was standing in a classroom in front of a group of eighth-grade students. I was there to tell them about my life. I am a Holocaust survivor. As a Jewish person born in Poland in the 1930s, I bore witness to the Nazis' attempt to eradicate all the Jews of Europe during World War II. At the start of 1939, there were about seven million Jewish people living in Central and Eastern Europe. By the war's end in 1945, an estimated six million of them had been killed, many in concentration camps like Bergen-Belsen and Dachau, and in death camps such as Treblinka and Auschwitz-Birkenau.

I survived the Holocaust because I was hidden by non-Jewish families who risked their lives to save the lives of others.

Though that part of my life happened many years ago, the memories are still fresh. I have made it one of my life's missions to tell my story, and to speak about the importance of tolerance, so that the atrocities of the past do not happen again. I travel across the country, speaking to students and teachers, at schools and synagogues, and meeting people from all different backgrounds. I also work as a gallery educator at the Museum of Jewish Heritage: A Living Memorial to the Holocaust in New York City. There, I give tours to groups of people and tell them my story too.

Whenever I talk to young people about my experiences, I find that all my memories from the past come back even stronger—my memories of suffering during the Holocaust, as well as the hope and joy and struggles that followed when the war ended and my family and I immigrated to America.

That spring day, standing in front of the eighth graders, I realized I wanted to write a memoir about what happened to me during the war but also about what happened when I came out of hiding—and slowly but surely, began to come back to life.

I hope that my story will help people understand the importance of remembering, and of treating each other with kindness and humanity.

1

Escaping Death

I SUPPOSE IT'S FITTING that I've had seven names, considering how many times I've had to restart my life.

On my birth certificate, I'm Aurelia Czeslava Gamzer. My Hebrew name is Rachel Tcharne, which I was given to honor both my late grandmother and great-aunt. During my early childhood, I was called Rela (short for Aurelia), then Relunia, then Lunia, and finally, Luncia, my favorite nickname, which stuck.

Luncia Gamzer was my name throughout my childhood and adolescence. Many years later, in a new country, my name would change again—to Ruth Gruener. But, of course, I didn't know it then.

I was born on a warm August morning in the early 1930s, in a house on Wolynska Street in the city of Lvov, which at that time was part of Poland. When I was six weeks old, I caught pneumonia and almost died. I was unconscious, but the doctor revived me by dunking me in basins of cold and warm water. That was the first time I escaped death. It would not be the last.

I was a happy child, with wavy brown hair cut in a short bob just under my ears and wide, bright hazel eyes. I didn't have any siblings, but I had lots of friends who lived nearby. We'd meet up to play tag or jump rope, and we'd stay out until our mothers called us in to dinner. I loved to dance and play songs on my pink toy piano and pick out ice cream from the chocolate shop, called Sarotina, that my parents,

Barbara and Isaac Gamzer, owned. We were Jewish, and I knew that made us different from many of our neighbors who celebrated Christmas while we observed holidays like Hanukkah and Rosh Hashanah (the Jewish New Year). Still, I always felt at home in Lvov.

But the world around me was changing fast. A tyrant named Adolf Hitler had taken over as the leader of Germany. Hitler blamed all of Germany's problems on Jewish people. He was determined to conquer all of Europe and make it *Judenrein*—free of Jews. In November 1938 in Germany, more than 8,000 Jewish homes, businesses, and synagogues were ransacked. Jewish people were beaten and shot in public places, and many were taken away to camps. This became known as Kristallnacht, or Night of Broken Glass.

I was five years old when Germany invaded Poland, marking the beginning of World War II. I'll never forget the morning that the German army marched into Lvov. Air raid sirens blared, followed by the sound of military planes and the smell of diesel fuel. Then came the whine of falling bombs and explosions.

"What is that noise?" I asked my father, confused and frightened. "I'm scared."

"I won't let anything happen to you," he said, and swooped me up in his arms. "But we need to hurry."

Tatu ("Father" in Polish) held me against his chest while he bounded down the stairs with Mama right behind us. Down in the cellar, I was terrified, but my father calmed me by telling me stories; he said that in heaven, there was a village where dolls could talk and walk on their own. I was transfixed; at that young age, I loved dolls, and the idea of seeing them walk and talk made me feel much less afraid. If I had to go to heaven, I reasoned, maybe it would be all right.

We spent days in the cellar until the bombing stopped. We came out of the cellar to learn that the Russian army had successfully fought off the Germans and entered Lvov. Life under the Russians was difficult. But in 1941, things got much, much worse. The German army came back to fight again, and this time, they won.

Under the German occupation, the calculated mass extermination of the more than 200,000 Jews in Lvov began. It's remarkable how clearly you can see the truth in hindsight but not as it's happening in the moment.

First, there were small changes in the city. Suddenly, Jews were not allowed to go to school, so I had to stay home, not quite understanding why. Also, Jewish people had to wear white armbands with a blue Star of David, so we could be easily identified. Having a dirty armband could get you in trouble, so my mother opted for the plastic cuff kind that easily wiped clean. The Star of David was such a beautiful symbol—one traditionally worn by Jews to signify God's protection—and the Nazis' use of it tainted its meaning. I hated wearing my armband, but I knew I had to have it on whenever I went outside.

It was all so strange. Why were we being persecuted, just for being Jewish? Only a short time ago, we had been equals in our community. So many of our non-Jewish neighbors, who had once respected us and been kind to us, were being brainwashed into turning against us. I could see it in the nasty, disapproving looks they shot us on the street and could feel it like a chill in the air.

And it felt like there was nothing we could do.

Every day it seemed there was a new rule. Jewish families were told to gather all their gold and silver and bring it to the synagogue to be confiscated. I looked on sadly as my mother took the silver candlesticks off our mantel. I knew they had belonged to my great-grandmother, and we'd used them to light the Shabbos candles every Friday night. Shabbos is the Sabbath, the Jewish day of rest, which begins on Friday evening and lasts until

Saturday evening. The beginning of Shabbos is marked by lighting candles and saying prayers over challah bread and wine. It's such a sweet, peaceful time, but now it felt as if we were losing some of that peace.

Next, we were told to turn in our furs. I remember my mother removing the gray fur lining from my favorite dark red winter coat and hat, and I felt a pang of sadness. It was only a coat and hat, but I was starting to understand that things were changing in a terrible way. After the fur went the furniture. The Nazis would break into people's homes and carry whatever they wanted—tables and chairs—onto trucks waiting in the street.

Jewish businesses were forced to close, so my parents had to shutter their chocolate shop, which was a terrible blow. We began to run out of money for food, so we resorted to eating boiled potatoes.

One afternoon, as my mother was boiling potatoes for dinner, a German soldier burst through the door.

My mother gasped at the sight of him, and my eyes got wide and I froze completely still.

"Give me all your gold and silver. Now!" he barked at my mother. "And you better not tell me you don't have any, because I know you must have saved some somewhere."

"But we've already given it all up," my mother pleaded. "We have nothing left."

The soldier stomped over to me, and he smelled like a mix of cologne, cigarettes, and liquor. I thought for sure he would kill me, but before I even knew what was happening, he reached his hands into the two pockets of my skirt to see if there was anything hidden. When he realized there wasn't, he turned to my mother.

"Fine," he said. "Give me that pot on the stove. It must be worth quite a bit."

I watched my mother put the half-boiled potatoes on a plate and wash the pot for the soldier. When he left, my mother said that she'd heard the Germans needed metal for war materials.

Soon the hum of anxiety turned to cold, raw fear. Our lives became harder. Scarier. I began to hear whispers about burning synagogues and about Nazis randomly stopping people on the street to ask for identification papers. If those people were Jewish, the Nazis would shoot them.

Then came a new rule: All Jews were ordered to live in one section of the city—an area my parents and I lived in already. But that meant we had to share our apartment with other families. Having to give up my room was another thing that made my life feel much less normal.

"But they're strangers!" I cried to my parents. "And why *my* room? Where will I put my dresses?" I knew I sounded spoiled, but I didn't care.

"Because we have no choice, Luncia," Tatu said, trying to calm me down. He ran his hand through his dark brown hair and crinkled his kind brow. "I'll run a rope across the corner of the room. You can hang your clothes there. On the plus side, you'll get to look at your dresses all the time."

Tatu always found a way to put a positive spin on things. At least, he did when he spoke to me. At night, when my parents thought I was sleeping, I would hear them whispering to each other.

"The Nazis are never going to stop until they've taken everything," Tatu said. "First all our possessions, then our home—and maybe even our lives." That last part chilled me to the bone.

Soon after, there came rumors of an *akzia*, which is the Polish word for "deportation." Jews would be loaded onto trucks and train cars, then taken away to camps—and killed.

The first *akzia* was for children.

The other child living in our apartment was a boy named Henio, who was older than me but scrawny, with dirty-blond hair that stuck up every which way. Henio acted like a big brother, and I came to love having him in my home.

For days we knew the *akzia* was going to happen,

but we didn't know exactly when. Tatu built me and Henio a hiding place by taking off the bathroom door and pushing a large wardrobe in front of it. Tatu cut a hole in the back of the wardrobe big enough for me and Henio to fit through. My mother hung clothes inside to cover the opening.

The morning of the *akzia*, we were woken up by the shrieks of women and children outside. There was no time to think. Feeling dizzy and nauseous, I quickly climbed through the wardrobe with Henio. The two of us crouched inside the bathroom, holding hands with our eyes squeezed shut tight. I bit down hard on a piece of cloth to prevent my teeth from chattering out of nerves.

Suddenly, we heard the heavy boots of a Nazi soldier inside our apartment. Terror gripped me. I heard the soldier's booming voice ask my parents a question in Polish, and I realized he was asking them about their daughter. *Their daughter! Me.* That's when it hit me: There was a photograph of me as a young child, in pajamas, hanging on the wall. Because of that picture, the soldier would realize that there *was* a child who lived in the apartment.

But then I heard Tatu answer in a strong, emotional voice: "She was already taken away." A lie, told to protect me.

"You had a pretty little girl," the Nazi replied. *Had.* Past tense. So he assumed I was dead.

I hoped he would leave after that, but he didn't. Henio and I froze as we heard his boots approaching our hiding place. He shone his flashlight toward the back of the wardrobe, and I held my breath. I was sure the Nazi would see that there was a hiding spot there—that *we* were in there. And I'm not sure why, but the soldier didn't investigate further. He turned his flashlight around and left the apartment.

Once again, I had avoided certain death. I was safe. But for how much longer?

2

The Ghetto

I LAY ALONE ON the floor of the office where my father worked. It was impossible to stay warm. No matter how I tried to bury myself in my clothes, some part of my body was exposed to the frigid air. The condensation of my breath hung above me as I exhaled. There was no way I could sleep.

Spending the night alone in an empty office had not been part of the plan. But then again, everything that had happened over the past year was unexpected. Unimaginable, actually.

All the Jewish people in Lvov—including my family, of course—had been forced to move to the ghetto, a rural area on the outskirts of the city. My parents and I had to say good-bye to Henio and his parents, who were also going to the ghetto—we never saw them again. We borrowed a wheelbarrow and put in a few pieces of clothing, a pot, and some dishes—all we could bring with us to move.

The ghetto was dingy and gray, full of stray cats and dogs and people on the sidewalks begging for food. My family and I were lucky to at least be able to live in a small room. But food in the ghetto was scarce, and we were constantly hungry.

The ghetto was surrounded by barricades topped with barbed wire. The Nazis had us trapped. They controlled who came in and out through a single gate. The only people allowed to leave the ghetto were those who worked outside. People who were nervous and took too long to show their identity cards were shot. Guard dogs were trained to attack and kill when given the command "Jew."

The ghetto seemed like a place that no one could escape. But earlier that day, I had done just that. I had wrapped my arms and legs tightly around my father's leg, hidden by his long overcoat. Tatu had a special card so he could leave the ghetto to go work in an office. His card said *"Nutzlicher Jude,"* which translates to "Useful Jew." With me tucked silently inside his coat, Tatu showed his card to the guards, and we made it outside.

My father had smuggled me out of the ghetto because I was about to go into hiding.

The day before, while walking to work, Tatu had run into a woman named Mrs. Szczygiel.

Mrs. Szczygiel and her husband, who were not Jewish, had been friends with my parents since I was a baby. They had three daughters of their own. The family often came into my parents' chocolate shop, and I later found out that they didn't have a lot of money for treats. When my father noticed the girls gazing longingly at the chocolates, he would let them pick out whatever they wanted for free. Other times, when Mrs. Szczygiel came by the shop to buy the tiny treats she *could* afford, she'd come home to find that my parents had also tucked a few expensive chocolates into her bag. Mrs. Szczygiel never forgot my parents' kindness.

When she saw my father outside the ghetto, she approached Tatu, greeted him, and said plainly: "I assume you, your wife, and your child will be killed. I want to save your daughter's life. Tomorrow, when you go to work, take Luncia with you. I will pick her up from your office and bring her to my home."

My parents and I had heard rumors that some Christian families were risking their lives to hide Jews in their homes. I couldn't believe that now I would be one of those hidden people. I hated the thought of being separated from my parents. But my parents insisted it would be for the best, even as my mother wept in front of me.

So now I was here, in my father's office, waiting for Mrs. Szczygiel. She was supposed to have arrived to pick me up earlier that day, but apparently she'd changed her mind at the last minute, worried about the risks of hiding me. One of Tatu's coworkers went to tell her that I had already escaped the ghetto. Thankfully, she reconsidered and agreed to come back to the office the following day. That's why I had to spend the night there, alone.

As I shivered on the freezing floor, I thought about my parents, anxious about what would happen to them while we were apart.

What I couldn't know was that a few weeks later, my father ran into a man named Mr. Oyak outside the ghetto. Mr. Oyak and his wife were not Jewish, and they had worked at my parents' chocolate shop before it closed. My father explained to Mr. Oyak that he and my mother had put me into hiding in the hope that I would survive the war. Tatu then asked Mr. Oyak if *he* might be willing to hide my mother.

And Mr. Oyak agreed, saying, "You are not only my boss; you are my best friend." The Oyaks took in my mother. And then later, when a rumor circulated that all the Jews who worked at my father's office would be shot, the Oyaks hid my father too.

And, eventually, me.

But that night in my father's office, I only knew fear. I couldn't bear the thought of losing my parents, of never seeing them again.

I knew that all of our extended family, who had also been living in the ghetto, were very likely dead. There had been *akzia*s in the ghetto too. Thinking back to everything that had unfolded during the weeks before made me shudder in the empty room.

My uncle Hirsch had lived with his wife, Clara, my cousins Fancia and Ben, as well as my grandmother, in a small room not too far from us in the ghetto. It was an early evening when my uncle came flying through the door, out of breath. He was whiter than the snow piled up along the barricades.

"I—I—I—" he stammered. "I shouldn't have run. I should have held her for one more moment. She . . ." He trailed off.

"What is it, Hirsch? What's going on?" Tatu said, taking my uncle's shoulders and moving him over to sit on some boxes in our makeshift kitchen. "Is it Clara? The children?"

Uncle Hirsch sat bent over with his head in his hands. He was tall and handsome, with broad shoulders and dark hair. Now he looked shrunken.

"Clara," he finally said. "She's dead."

My heart stopped.

Uncle Hirsch explained that earlier that day, there'd been an *akzia*, and he and Clara had been forced onto a truck by soldiers. The truck had stopped in a clearing and the soldiers had shot all the passengers—but my uncle had managed to escape. My aunt had not been so lucky.

My parents and I stood silent for what felt like ages, until my mother spoke.

"Where are Fancia and Ben, and Grandma?" Mama asked. Her voice had a quiet strength.

"Home," my uncle managed to say. "I hope."

"Go be with your children," Tatu said. "They need you now more than ever." So Uncle Hirsch left.

There was another *akzia* a few days later. My father had dug a hiding place underneath our front porch. It was like a little cave. There was hardly enough room for my parents and me, but it would have to do. The *akzia* was rumored to start early the following morning—and last for several days. My mother, my father, and I climbed inside the little cave at dawn, and before too long, we heard trucks and people wailing in the street. The sound of an *akzia*.

Just then came two familiar voices yelling.

"Aunt Barbara, Uncle Isaac!" the voices called over and over again. I froze. It was my cousins Fancia and Ben.

My first instinct was to unscrunch myself and bolt out, but I felt my mother press me down.

"No, Luncia," she breathed, throwing her arm across me. "We can't. There's no room."

"But we can't just let them die!" I whispered. Tears were streaming down my cheeks.

"If we went out to get them, we would be captured and die too," Tatu said. "There's nothing we can do."

How could this be happening? My mind raced with terror at the thought of my cousins being taken away. My mother held me close and put her hand to my forehead, trying to keep me calm.

When the *akzia* was over and it was safe to come out, the ghetto was eerily quiet. I ran to the room where my relatives had lived—and it was empty. I screamed out in horror. My grandmother, my uncle, and my cousins were all gone.

It was just me and my parents left—but now we had been separated too. I wasn't sure how I could survive on my own.

I didn't think I would ever fall asleep there on the cold office floor, but I must have drifted off. The next day, Mrs. Szczygiel came to get me. I was eight years old, and my life in hiding was about to begin.

3

Hidden

I WAS INCONSOLABLE MY first few days at the Szczygiels'—not that there was anyone to console me. I was all alone most of the day, sitting still as a statue on the small burgundy settee in the corner of a back bedroom. The rules were that I had to remain on that small couch and not move or make any noise. So I sobbed uncontrollably in silence. I'd cry into one handkerchief, then lay it flat to dry while I cried into another.

All I could think about was my parents. I'd ask

myself questions I couldn't answer: *Was there another* akzia*? Did my mother go into hiding? Did Tatu take too long to find his identity card at the ghetto's gate and get attacked by a guard dog?* These thoughts would send a chill down the middle of my back.

There was nothing to distract me either. I wasn't allowed to get up unless I had to use the little potty, which I'd slide out from under the sofa and push back after I went.

Mr. and Mrs. Szczygiel and their three daughters, Jasia, Hela, and Marisia, all left early in the morning to go to work and school. Mrs. Szczygiel's mother, who I eventually came to call Babcia ("Grandma" in Polish), took care of my basic needs. She would bring me bread to eat and tea-flavored water to drink.

"*Shhh!* Too loud!" Babcia would scold whenever I spoke. "You must whisper! The walls are thin and neighbors will hear. And walk on your tiptoes! The family downstairs will get suspicious if they hear an extra pair of feet thudding on the floor."

If someone found out that the Szczygiels were hiding a Jewish person in their house, and reported them to the Nazis, the whole family would be killed. And I would be killed too, of course.

That was also why I was absolutely not allowed to *ever* go near the window. A neighbor across the street might spot me.

So I sat in my cold, dark corner—Mrs. Szczygiel kept off the lights and heat to save money—and nobody talked to me or even looked in my direction. I was like a nonperson. A body that took up space. I was so lonely. There weren't any books to read, or any papers and pencils to draw with. To keep myself sane, I silently told myself stories— the fairy tales my mother used to tell me before I went to bed. I'd go over them in my mind from beginning to end, trying to remember every detail.

And often, I'd pray. I didn't really know any prayers, so I began to speak to God as a friend—a best friend. "Please help me," I would whisper. "Please help me." And somehow that made me feel a little better.

Sometimes during those long cold days, I'd catch myself dozing off, and what usually woke me up was the feeling of my head sliding down the wall.

The evening, after dinner, was the only part of my day that distracted me. The three Szczygiel sisters would sit at a beautiful mahogany dressing table on the opposite side of the room. They'd ignore me, but I'd watch as they curled their hair and tried on makeup. I both wanted their attention and hated them for having the life I couldn't. Their activities reminded me that I too once fussed with my hair and clothes, and that there had been a time when all that had occupied my thoughts were school and friends.

I'll never have that again, I'd tell myself in my

darkest moments. I knew that I was feeling sorry for myself. *Why shouldn't I feel sorry for myself?* I'd hear myself answer. *I've lost everything, and even if I manage to survive this war, there will be no going back to my old life.*

One day, when Mr. and Mrs. Szczygiel and the girls were away at work and school, I sat on the couch, staring at that mahogany dressing table. My boredom and frustration reached a breaking point. So, even though I knew it was against the rules, I stood up and tiptoed over to the dressing table. That table was especially forbidden, because it was near the window.

But I held my breath, quietly slid the stool out from underneath the table, and sat down. I began opening the jars and bottles of makeup and putting different creams on my face. Soon enough I tired of this activity. It seemed as if the Szczygiel girls had more fun sitting there than I did. I realized it had less to do with putting on makeup and more about spending time together. So I stood up and tiptoed back to my spot on the couch.

Later that day, Mrs. Szczygiel came into the room to get something out of the closet. When she looked at me and saw my bright red face, she cried, "Mother! Come! This child is burning up with fever!" Babcia came running in and slapped her hand to my forehead so hard that she nearly knocked my head against the wall. She looked perplexed to find that my head was cool, and then turned to fix her eyes on the dressing table. I looked over and realized I had forgotten to put the cover back on one of the jars. It was clear that my face was only red because I'd painted it with creams and makeup. When Mrs. Szczygiel realized what Babcia had discovered, the two women burst out laughing. I was shocked and relieved that neither of them yelled at me for what I'd done.

But the next day, one of the neighbors who lived in the building across the street saw Mrs. Szczygiel at the market. She asked who the young girl was she saw through the bedroom window. When Mrs. Szczygiel came home, she was furious.

"Luncia, what's the matter with you?" she snapped. I shivered. I knew I was in deep trouble. "I had to make up a story on the spot about my niece coming to visit. And I'm sure she thought I was lying and she's going to report me, and then we'll all be finished!"

"I'm really sorry," I said, but she had already stormed away.

The family's anxiety about my presence was getting higher. It came to a head when Mr. Szczygiel found out the building's apartments were being painted.

"What are we going to do with the girl?" Mr. Szczygiel asked his wife after dinner one evening.

That was what they called me: the girl.

"Well, she can't stay in the apartment during the

day, obviously," Mrs. Szczygiel said. "We'll have to hide her."

Their solution was to put me out with the trash. Mr. Szczygiel placed me inside a burlap sack and carried me to the basement of their building. I spent the day down there, watching rats and mice scurry around. In the evening, after the painters left, Mr. Szczygiel would pick me up in the sack, throw me over his shoulder, and bring me back upstairs. This went on for two days, and somehow, miraculously, the ruse worked.

Then, one day, something much worse happened. One of the daughters, Marisia, got sick and stayed home from work. She spent the day in the bedroom with me, sleeping, but in the late afternoon, her coworker Alex came to see her. No one could give me any warning, so when I saw the doorknob turn, I jumped up from my spot on the couch and barely had time to slide under the bed.

The problem was, the Szczygiels had a little dog, a

Chihuahua named Jockey. He was the light of Mrs. Szczygiel's life, and she was more affectionate with him than she was with her own family. That afternoon, Jockey was in the room with us too, and as soon as I went under the bed, he started barking; he thought I was playing a game. I lay frozen in terror, praying that Marisia's friend wouldn't notice me. Alex kept glancing down toward where I was, to see what Jockey was barking at, and Marisia kept trying to get him to look out the window by asking him what the weather was like. Thankfully, just when I thought for sure Alex would discover me, Mrs. Szczygiel came into the room and Jockey immediately ran toward her. I let out a breath of relief, trembling.

That was the last straw. After Alex left, Marisia and her sisters begged their parents for me to leave. In many ways, I understood why they wanted me gone, but it made me feel scared and helpless.

The girls' father agreed with them. I overheard

Mr. Szczygiel say to Babcia that it wasn't fair for them to sacrifice six lives for one. But what could they do with me?

Babcia and Mrs. Szczygiel came up with an idea—they would hide me from the rest of the family.

"Get in," Babcia said to me one day, pointing to a long, narrow trunk. It looked like a coffin. She and Mrs. Szczygiel had cut a small hole in the side of the trunk so I could breathe. Babcia handed me a wet rag. "Put this over your nose and mouth," she instructed. "There's oxygen in the water. It'll help you breathe."

For three weeks, I climbed into my coffin every night before the rest of the family came home, and only climbed out in the morning after they'd left. Often, I'd be trapped in my coffin for twelve-hour stretches. After a little while, my legs and arms would go numb. As the feeling in my body slipped away, I'd start to panic because I would literally feel like I was dying.

One morning, Marisia happened to lean on the trunk, and she felt me move inside. She screamed and jumped off. Mrs. Szczygiel and Babcia's secret was up.

I went back to hiding in plain sight in my spot on the couch, waiting for the moment I might be caught and taken away by the Nazis.

Then, one day, Mrs. Szczygiel came running into the room and blurted out four life-changing words.

"Your parents are alive!" she nearly shouted. "I met Mrs. Oyak at the market, and she told me that your father and mother managed to escape the ghetto. Your mother went into hiding with Mr. and Mrs. Oyak first, and your father followed about a month later."

For the first time in ages, I felt a rush of hope. Knowing that my parents were all right and living not far away gave me new strength.

And best of all, Mrs. Szczygiel said she would be taking me to the Oyaks' so I could *see* my parents. I wasn't sure if it meant that the Oyaks would take me in too—I assumed there wasn't room for me—or if Mrs. Szczygiel was lying about the whole thing and would abandon me in the street when we went outside. But I knew I had to have faith.

After weeks of living in the trunk, I had forgotten how to walk properly. And after eight months in hiding, only allowed to whisper, I'd forgotten how to speak in an audible voice. I sounded like a rooster crowing. There was no way I could leave the apartment until I could reverse these two things, or else someone on the street might suspect something strange about me.

Babcia began to teach me how to walk and speak properly again. She'd lead me by my arm, reminding me to bend my knees as we walked back and forth in back of the bedroom, far away from the window. It was much harder than I'd imagined.

"I can't keep going, Babcia," I'd say to her after a short time. "I'm tired."

"You have to keep going if you're going to get strong enough to go outside," she said. "How would it look if a young girl such as yourself didn't have a spring in her step?"

After my walking lesson, she'd sit me on the couch and, so no one would hear me, wrap my face with a thick scarf and make me repeat words out loud. All my words would come out sounding like I was underwater, but we practiced for a few days until she decided I'd made enough progress.

Finally, the day came for me to leave. Mrs. Szczygiel tried to make me look as presentable as possible, but I'd grown since going into hiding, and the only decent dress I owned was short on me. My shoes were so tight that I begged Mrs. Szczygiel to let me leave them unlaced, but she said it was too risky, and so I squeezed my feet inside and tied them up.

Mrs. Szczygiel and I walked down the stairs and into the street. I had not been outside for eight months. Blinded by the bright sunshine, I closed my eyes and let the warmth of the sun envelop my entire body. Slowly, opening one eye at a time, my gaze fell on a tree. It was so green, and its beautifully shaped leaves gently fluttered in the summer breeze. I looked up and saw a perfectly blue sky, dotted with small white clouds that looked just like feathers spilling out of a torn pillow. I heard birds chirping nearby. Pink, red, and purple flowers were blooming in the window box of a blue house. All the colors around me were intensely vibrant, and it seemed as if I were seeing everything for the very first time.

We took a bus to Zielona Street, where the Oyaks lived. When we arrived, we knocked on the apartment door, and Mr. Oyak opened it. Behind him, I saw Mama and Tatu rush toward me. *They were alive.* The three of us embraced, and my parents covered me with kisses.

"I thought I would never see you again!" I sobbed. "I—I—" I stammered. I had so many emotions welling up, I hardly knew what to say. I remembered everything

I had seen—the sky, the birds, the flowers—when I'd walked outside for the first time that day. Finally, I blurted: "The world is so beautiful. I want so much to live."

For a moment, I thought I'd said something wrong because my parents started to cry. The Oyaks and Mrs. Szczygiel began to cry too.

I later learned that Mr. Oyak was so moved by my words that he knew on the spot he couldn't let me go. His voice choking up, Mr. Oyak said, "Let Luncia stay here with us. It's the same death whether I am hiding one, two, or three Jews."

So I began my life in hiding with the Oyaks, but now I had my parents, at least. That made everything better.

My parents and I hid in the Oyaks' common room; my parents slept on a cot in the corner and I slept on the table. Food was scarce, so we were hungry and cold all the time, and we had to live in silence, the way I had at the Szczygiels'.

At that point, I had only one pair of socks to wear, and they were full of holes. It was important to wear socks in the house so that my footsteps would be silent when I walked. So my mother used an old pair of her stockings to reinforce the soles of my ragged socks. And because the socks were so dirty and gray after so much time, my mother borrowed some navy ink from Mrs. Oyak to dye the socks and make them look nicer. It was the little things that made a difference.

But eventually, the atmosphere at the Oyaks' became stressful. There were too many of us in close quarters. My parents felt bad that we were such a burden to the family. Once, I overheard my mother and Mrs. Oyak casually discussing ways we could end our lives.

"We could take poison," my mother suggested.

"But what would we do with your bodies?" Mrs. Oyak said.

My mother considered this. "I suppose," she said, "there's no place to burn us."

"True," Mrs. Oyak answered. Then she had an idea.

"One of Mrs. Szczygiel's daughters has a boyfriend who's an undercover officer with the Polish police," she began. "Maybe we could find out if he would be willing to take you all into the woods and shoot you."

I listened in horror to everything they said—they didn't know it, but I had my ear to the bedroom door, hearing every word. A white haze filled my eyes, creeping in from the corners until it clouded my vision, and the room started to spin.

How could they be planning our deaths like it's everyday conversation? I thought wildly. *We're human beings! And we've gotten this far. What if we're killed and the war ends the next day? That would be a tragedy!*

None of it felt real.

But it was real. Plans were made for the executioner to come the following Tuesday at dusk.

That Tuesday, the day I was going to die, I felt

as if my arms and legs—my whole body—were engulfed in flames. My parents and I didn't speak about what was going to happen to us.

The sun went down, and the chilly air penetrated the room we were sitting in. With every moment that passed, I felt myself grow more and more anxious. Every time I heard footsteps on the staircase, my heart would drop into my feet. I started to watch the clock on the wall. Five o'clock came and went. Then six o'clock. With rising terror, I climbed into my mother's lap and began pulling on her clothes and scratching at her chest, desperate to hide myself, to do something.

"I'm scared," I said over and over again. "I'm scared. I'm scared. I'm scared."

I think this was the most frightening moment of my life.

Then it was seven o'clock. I was afraid to breathe. I kept my eyes on the clock and watched the minute hand move forward. Seven fifteen, seven thirty. I strained to listen to any footsteps in the hallway, but it was very quiet. Our executioner never came.

The next day, Mrs. Szczygiel came over and told us that her daughter's boyfriend decided he couldn't do it. He wasn't a killer. My parents and I let out our breath. Maybe, just maybe, we would live to see the end of the war.

4

Liberation

IT WAS LATE JULY 1944—hot and sticky inside the Oyaks' apartment. I couldn't sleep well; I kept tossing and turning on the table. Finally, I woke up in the morning to commotion. I heard everyone rushing around the room and sat bolt upright. My mother hurried over to me in a flurry and grabbed my shoulders.

"Luncia!" she cried. "We're being liberated! The Russians are taking back the city and the Germans are leaving!"

I looked at my father. "Is it true, Tatu?" I asked.

It was. The Russian army had liberated Lvov with help from the Polish Resistance, an underground organization that worked with the Allied forces to fight the Nazis. We had known from listening to the radio that the Allies—which included the United States and Great Britain—were slowly retaking cities across Europe, and that the German army was being defeated. The war wasn't over yet, but thankfully, Lvov was now free.

"But we shouldn't go outside right away," my mother said, looking at my father. "What if the Germans come back?"

Mr. and Mrs. Oyak agreed it was best to be cautious and wait it out. So we did.

After a few days, it became clear that the Nazi occupation *had* really ended. Our five-year nightmare was over.

My father decided to go out first. He left the apartment and was outside for a while. My mother and I waited anxiously for him inside. When Tatu came back, he told us what had happened. It was a story that still stays with me until this day.

Out in the street, my father saw a damaged German tank. Sitting inside the tank was a very young, very badly wounded German soldier. The soldier was holding his wounded arm and crying. People had gathered around the tank, looking at the soldier without sympathy. My father walked over to see what was happening.

"I didn't do anything," the young soldier sobbed. "I was drafted into the army. I didn't even want to fight. Please, please, somebody get me a doctor."

My father, who was a self-taught man, was the only one in the crowd who spoke German. And he was the only one who went over to the soldier to speak to him.

"Calm down," my father told the soldier. "I'll ask someone to phone an ambulance for you. And I will stay with you until the ambulance arrives."

People in the crowd saw that my father was speaking to the soldier, and they began to scream at Tatu.

"How could you?" they yelled. "He's a German! He's our enemy! He came here to kill us!"

And of course anyone could understand why the people felt this way, after all the horrors that had happened.

But my father remained resolute. "He's young," my father explained to the angry crowd. "He doesn't want to kill anybody. And he needs help."

Finally, someone in the crowd agreed to go back to their house and call for an ambulance. My father stayed with the wounded German soldier until the ambulance came and took the soldier away.

After my father finished telling this story, I was quiet. I wasn't sure I would have been able to show the same sympathy and bravery that my father had. But he helped me understand how important it is to not hate an entire group of people. Everyone is an individual, and deserving of dignity, and while there is evil in the world, there is always goodness too. I'm so grateful to my father for this lesson.

At last, the day came when I too was able to go outside. As my parents got ready to go, I realized I only had my old dyed socks to wear on my feet—but they didn't fit anymore. And I certainly had no shoes that fit. I started to cry, feeling all the frustration and pain well up in me. Mrs. Oyak saw my tears and handed me a pair of her old slippers, which were made of straw. I stuffed my feet inside the slippers, and my parents and I finally left the building.

My legs were jiggly from not walking enough, and my parents helped me along the street.

After walking for a little while, I began to feel very warm, and my eyes kept wanting to close. I wasn't used to the direct sunlight. My mother took out a pair of sunglasses from her bag and put them on my nose; the dark lenses instantly helped me see better.

What I saw across the street was a woman walking with two girls about my age. I stopped and stared at them. It had been so long since I'd seen other children.

I looked all around. The city's beautiful buildings were still standing, but doors were off their hinges or missing altogether, and the facades were in disrepair. Rubble and debris such as pieces of equipment and torn clothing filled the streets.

Suddenly, my body felt tired and achy. It was hard to put one foot in front of the other.

"I'm taking her back," my mother announced to Tatu. "Luncia needs to regain her strength. She can barely stand on her own. It's enough for her for one day."

The wave of exhaustion was so intense that I didn't even fight my mother on it. Otherwise, I could have kept walking until the streets and ornate buildings glowed in the golden light of sunset. Before the war, I had taken so much of Lvov's beauty for granted, and now there were so many people who would never see this beauty again.

⁊⁊

Within a few days, my mother found us an available three-room apartment in a building on the same street as the Oyaks. The building's caretaker told my mother that a German family had lived there and fled the city after the occupation ended. The apartment was fully furnished, right down to the utensils in the drawers.

"I told him that we had lost all our possessions," Mama said, relaying the conversation she had had with the building's caretaker to Tatu and me. "I told him we just want to start a normal life, even though we don't yet have the money to pay rent. He said we can pay him when we are able, and that we can move in whenever we are ready."

My parents and I settled into the new place quickly, but none of us could shake the feeling of being on edge every waking second. We couldn't let go of thinking that a Nazi was going to burst through the door at any moment and kill us. It would be a long time before that fear would go away.

I didn't feel any safer after a week of living in our new apartment, but I did start remembering what it was like to have my own space. My bedroom had a mirror, and now I was free to walk over to it. I had caught glimpses of myself while I was in hiding but hadn't given myself a good hard stare in a long time. Same wavy brown hair—longer now. Same wide-set eyes. But I felt so different inside. *Who is this person looking back at me?* I thought. I didn't know what my new life was going to be like. All I knew was that it was going to be very different from the one I had before.

Back when my parents were in the ghetto, my father put several of our family photographs into a glass jar and buried them in a safe place. Once we were liberated, he was able to go back to the spot where he'd buried the photos—and miraculously, they were still there, untouched: photos of me as a baby, photos of my parents, even the photo of me that had hung on the wall when the Nazi soldier almost caught me hiding behind the wardrobe. I knew we would treasure those photos always.

I was grateful for what we had. We had survived the Holocaust and were restarting our lives. But it was difficult not to think about all we had lost.

There was nothing left for us in Poland. The rest of our family in Europe had died at the hands of the Nazis. The only family we had left lived in America—in New York City. They were Uncle Joseph and my cousins Izzy, Leon, and Helen; Uncle Abe and Aunt Ida and my cousin David; and my uncle Benny and Aunt Rebecca. They had all immigrated to America many years before I was born. My parents decided that we should leave Europe as soon as possible and make our way to America too.

My parents and I were called "displaced persons,"

or "DPs" for short. There were hundreds of thousands of DPs after the war, Europeans who had lost their homes and families. Many of the DPs like me and my family wanted to go to America. A mass exodus of displaced persons would soon begin. The journey would be grueling. There was no telling who would be granted a visa to legally enter the United States. There were no assurances, no definitive timeline. The application process was complicated and confusing. We knew it would take a long time, but we didn't know how long. It could be a year, three years, five years—it was anyone's guess. And there was always the possibility of getting a visa and embarking on the two-week trip across the Atlantic Ocean only to be told once you arrived that you had to turn around and go back.

But my parents had to hope we would make it there. Although we were still living in Lvov, the process of our immigration was slowly beginning.

5

Surprises

I HELD MY HEAD in my hand and my composition book was propped up on my arm. I couldn't stop my thoughts from wandering. Throughout my morning tutoring session, I kept losing my place while I was reading and stumbling over words.

"Did you forget to eat breakfast, Luncia?" Miss Lewicka, my tutor, finally asked me. I took my nose out of my book and stared at her wide-eyed.

"You aren't concentrating like you always do."

Uh-oh. She noticed.

"Um, yes, I ate," I said, trying to think up an excuse. "I don't think I slept very well last night. I mean, I had trouble falling asleep, so I'm a little tired."

I felt bad for lying. I wasn't very good at it anyway.

All the schools in Lvov were still closed after the war, so my parents had hired a tutor for me. That way, I'd be prepared for starting school in America. Miss Lewicka came to the apartment every day to give me lessons.

But that morning, my mind was far from my textbooks. I was thinking about what had happened the night before. My parents weren't able to reopen their shop, Sarotina, after the war, so they made small batches of candy in our apartment and sold it to pay the rent. If there was extra money at the end of the week, they'd often invite the Oyaks and the Szczygiels over for dinner.

The night before, something Mrs. Szczygiel said at the dinner table caught my attention.

"I couldn't believe it when she told me Jockey was a father!" she boomed. "My Jockey! With his own litter of puppies! I remember when he was a little puppy himself."

Jockey, Mrs. Szczygiel's beloved little Chihuahua, was the one who had almost given away my hiding place under the bed that scary night.

At dinner, I sat up straight, feeling a rush of excitement for the first time in ages.

Puppies?! I thought. *How many puppies? Do they have homes? Do I dare ask Mrs. Szczygiel or my parents if there are any left—and if I can have one?*

Lost in my thoughts, I'd missed a snippet of the conversation.

"You should see her," I heard Mrs. Szczygiel continue. "She's adorable! I named her Lala."

One puppy. A girl, named Lala. "Lala" means "doll" in Polish.

My mother was an expert mind reader—or she was with me, anyway. She was looking square at me, smiling. She knew what I was thinking: *I want that puppy!* I didn't say anything though. I had a feeling that asking for a puppy at this time in our lives would be too much trouble.

That's why I was so distracted the next day at my tutoring lesson. And I didn't do any better at my piano lesson later. Playing piano was something I had learned to do as a young girl, and I loved it. My parents had found a teacher in our apartment building to give me lessons. I was usually pretty good at piano, though that day I couldn't get my fingers to listen to my brain.

"Where is the young lady who played it so perfectly in my apartment all week?" my teacher asked after I messed up the piece for a third time.

Ugh.

After my lesson was done, I slowly climbed up the stairwell back to my apartment, feeling crushed by my day so far. I had just reached the landing below our floor when suddenly I heard a couple of yappy barks! I took the next set of stairs two by two and nearly dropped my piano books as I rounded the corner of the hall before throwing open my apartment door.

My mother and Mrs. Szczygiel were standing in the kitchen—and there was a tiny puppy in Mrs. Szczygiel's arms! I dropped my books on the floor as I gasped and covered my mouth. I was so happy!

Mrs. Szczygiel immediately passed Lala to me. The puppy's tiny paws splayed out in midair, and I caught her wriggling body in my arms. Her coat was smooth and she was mostly black but had caramel-colored hair at her throat. She was no bigger than one of my old favorite dolls—Mrs. Szczygiel had chosen the perfect name.

When I brought Lala to my chest, she licked my face and wouldn't stop barking.

"Quiet, Lala!" my mother said. "You'll annoy the neighbors!"

But I didn't care. I laughed and hugged Lala close. I realized that until that moment, I hadn't let myself feel true joy after being liberated. Lala was another step toward bringing me back to life.

My parents fell in love with Lala too. As much work as it was to have a puppy in the house, Lala always made us laugh and coo over how cute she was. She was a gift to us all.

Then something else wonderful happened. The dress I'd been wearing every day was stained and frayed, and at least two sizes too small. With the spare money we had, my mother bought me a new dress, simple but pretty. It wasn't glamorous and high-waisted like a woman's dress or a shapeless, cutesy A-line frock for a girl. It was somewhere in between.

For the first time in a long time, my life felt almost normal. The horror of the Holocaust finally felt like something that had happened in the past. I felt safe, and Lala was a big part of that. I still thought about the war, but I thought more about my future.

Just when that settled feeling started to take hold, it came to an abrupt end. We learned that the city of Lvov would no longer be part of Poland but rather of Soviet Ukraine. The Soviets decreed that all men and women had to work. My mother was notified that there was a job available for her, but far away—in Russia. She responded to the offer, saying she had a husband and child she didn't want to leave. The response came quickly: *You are young. You will soon have another husband and child here.*

My parents decided it was time to leave Lvov and go to a city called Kraków, which was still a part of Poland. But we'd have to move right away.

6

Good-Bye, Lvov

"LALA, ENOUGH!" I CRIED.

Bark, hop, *bark,* hop, in and out of our suitcases she leapt. Lala ran and nipped at my heels before jumping back into my suitcase. I couldn't help but forgive her for her antics.

"Oh, Lala," I said, lifting her out of a bag. "Don't worry. You're coming with us."

We were officially leaving for Kraków, a large city in southern Poland. My parents hoped that it would be easier to immigrate to America from there. With packing underway, our apartment became messy, and the flurry of activity made Lala excited. She ran around barking as if announcing to everyone within earshot that we were leaving.

"As long as you don't escape again," I told Lala, cuddling her close.

Lala had a bad habit of running out the apartment's front door and into the hallway, and we'd have to go calling after her to come back inside.

One morning a few days before, I was sitting on the floor with Mama, sorting our things. I suddenly realized that our apartment was very quiet. Too quiet.

"Have you seen Lala?" I asked my mother.

"Not in a little while," she answered. "Maybe Tatu went to take her for a walk?"

"No, Tatu is in the bedroom reading," I said.

My mother and I got up and started searching around. We lifted the piles of clothing out of the suitcases to see if Lala was curled up inside. She had grown, but she was still very little and liked to find cozy places to sleep. Except she wasn't in any of them.

"Lala!" my mother called around the apartment.

I started to panic. *Where could she be?* I looked for her under the table, in her favorite spot next to the radiator, and in the bathroom, where she sometimes slept behind the toilet. She was nowhere.

Then a shriek came from the hall. Tatu heard it too, and the three of us went running outside. A neighbor was standing at the top of the stairs, pointing to the ground floor three stories below.

"Your dog!" the woman exclaimed. "She fell from the top landing!"

My heart stopped and I froze, too shocked to react. If something had happened to Lala, I couldn't bear it. Tatu ran the fastest down the steps, but then we heard little paws click-clacking their way up. Lala and Tatu met halfway, and he scooped her up in his arms and carried her back up.

I ran over to my father and threw out my arms for

my puppy. She was okay, licking my hands as if nothing had happened.

"What would I have done if you had gotten hurt, you naughty girl!" I said, and nuzzled her face. Lala was everything to me, the source of almost all of my happiness. I couldn't imagine my life without her.

Finally, on moving day, we zipped up our suitcases and I picked up Lala. My parents and I said good-bye to the Szczygiels and the Oyaks. It was bittersweet and emotional. It was because of their kindness, generosity, and bravery that we had survived the Holocaust. What could we even say to thank them?

As my parents and I carried our suitcases to the train station, I looked around at the only place I ever knew and felt a little sad, wondering if I'd see Lvov again.

We boarded the train bound for Kraków. I held my breath as the train's whistle blew, and then we lurched forward and were on our way. As the train picked up speed, I started getting excited. *Will there be a school for me to go to instead of having a tutor? I bet Kraków has a library that's so big I won't be able to choose which books to borrow!* But deep down inside what I hoped for more than anything was the chance to make friends.

With my head leaning on the window, I watched the blurred landscape float by. Thinking about that big unknown made my stomach ache. I just wanted to have a normal life, and I knew that it would probably be a long time before that happened. I closed my eyes and let myself be lulled to sleep by the moving train.

7

Friends

MY OATMEAL WAS SO thick that I could make my spoon stand straight up inside the bowl. I started playing a game, seeing how far I could push the spoon without it toppling over.

"Luncia!" My mother startled me so that I accidentally launched the spoon into the air and it came down with a plop, spilling oatmeal on the table.

"Oops, sorry," I said sheepishly, retrieving the utensil from the other end of the table.

My neck was still sore from leaning on the train's

window all night. The trip to Kraków took almost an entire day, and when we arrived, I was exhausted and exhilarated all at once. Outside the station, I stood transfixed as people hurried past in fine-looking coats and new boots. I was also awed by the city's beautiful, pristine buildings. Unlike other major cities in Poland, such as Warsaw and Białystok, Kraków hadn't been destroyed by the Nazis. Looking around, you wouldn't know there had been a war.

Along with other Jewish families who were eventually heading for America, my parents and I were brought to a warehouse-like building that had been converted to simple, communal living quarters. I had learned there was an orphanage upstairs. This morning, I realized the orphanage might have potential new friends for me.

"Can't I go upstairs now?" I asked my mother, cleaning up my oatmeal spill.

"When you're finished eating, I'll go up with you," she said.

"Why do you have to take me? I'm old enough to go by myself."

My mother shot me her "don't even start" look. My parents had become so overprotective since the war ended. I felt like I was suffocating under their watch.

Finally, Mama and I went upstairs. In the orphanage, kids of all ages filled a large room. Everyone turned around as I stood in the doorway. My heart stopped. I was so nervous! I hadn't been around other kids in such a long time. I didn't know how to act or what to say. Then a dark-haired girl around my age skipped over.

"Hi, I'm Dora," she said, and thrust out her hand for me to shake. "And you are . . . ?"

"Luncia," I answered quickly, smiling. "Nice to meet you, Dora."

I glanced behind me. My mother had gone back downstairs. At least I didn't have to suffer the embarrassment of having one of my parents hovering close by.

"I've been here for about a month," Dora said. "Was that your mother?"

I felt uncomfortable talking about my mother, knowing that Dora's parents had died in the war. That's why she—and all the other kids here—were in the orphanage. I caught myself gazing down at my shoes and quickly looked up. I tried to sound cheerful.

"Yes, we just arrived last night," I said, and then blurted, "My father and my dog, Lala, too."

Then I felt even worse. Here I was, with not just a mother, but a father and a dog, and Dora had no family. I shifted from one foot to the other and awkwardly turned my head away from her.

"Oh, don't feel bad," Dora said. "I do miss my family terribly, but I really like it here. There's always someone to play with. We're in the middle of a game. Come join us."

Dora introduced me to all the other kids in the room. While we played games, we also spent time sharing stories of how we had survived the Holocaust. It may seem strange that we wanted to talk about that horrible time and dig up memories that were difficult and often painful. But sharing our experiences helped—a lot. We had all managed to live through circumstances no human being should have been forced to withstand. Even though our hearts were heavy because we had all lost people we loved, we were also uplifted by our collective strength. In a way, it made us feel almost invincible.

The Jewish organization that ran the orphanage started a school in the building. Though I was excited to be taking classes again—another step toward feeling normal—I'd forgotten how tiring school was. Sitting at a desk all day with only a short break for lunch was exhausting. And we had school six days a week. Saturday was our only day off. One day, walking to class, I became very dizzy and almost fell down the stairs. One of the teachers saw, and told my parents. She recommended I take a few days at home to rest. I wondered if in some ways I was still recovering from my time in hiding and adapting to this new reality.

But just when I started to adjust more, just when I began catching up with schoolwork and feeling like I'd made real friends in Kraków, a sudden change came again.

8

Good-Bye, Lala

I SAT ON MY bed and buried my face in Lala's fur, which was wet from my tears. Nothing my parents did or said to comfort me helped to stop my crying. I wasn't hungry and didn't feel like going upstairs to play with my friends. I sobbed and sobbed, feeling like my heart was breaking.

In a week, we would leave Kraków for a small town in Austria to stay at a displaced persons camp, then continue on to Munich, Germany. That would be our final stop in Europe before we could leave for

America. There was one problem, and it was a big one: Lala. We weren't allowed to take her with us. I was devastated. I couldn't imagine not having my puppy curled up on my pillow at night or hearing her happy barks when I got home. I started to feel unsafe and vulnerable again, like I shouldn't be too happy because something was bound to come along and take the happiness away.

What would I do without her? And where would she go?

My parents felt as bad as I did. We didn't want to leave her with just anyone.

"What about taking her back to the Szczygiels?" my mother suggested. "Then Lala will get to be with her father, Jockey."

I didn't want to admit it, but it was a good idea. As sad as I was, thinking about Lala being with Jockey made me feel better.

We packed up Lala's ratty blanket and her favorite toys. My mother made her a carrying case out of a box and string. Letting Lala out of my arms and putting her in the case was gut-wrenching. I didn't want to say good-bye.

My mother left to take Lala back to the Szczygiels, who at that time were living in a town called Wrocław. I tried to put on a brave face for Tatu, even though I missed Lala so much. We had to focus now on packing for Austria. And maybe it was time for me to start behaving more maturely. I sometimes felt so grown-up, and other times like a little kid.

When my mother came back from dropping off Lala, she and my father got busy finishing up the candy orders that they wanted to take care of before we left—my parents had continued their candy business in Kraków. One morning my mother was out dropping off orders, and I was home alone with my father. I woke up feeling strange—sort of heavy, with pain in my lower stomach. I didn't even want to get out of bed. I hoped I wasn't sick. Reluctantly, I swung my legs off the side of the bed, and stood up, and when I turned around to straighten my blanket, I saw a spot of blood on the sheet.

"Oh no!" I screamed. "Tatu, Tatu, come quick!"

He ran into the bedroom with a worried look on his face. "What is it, Luncia? What's wrong?"

"Look!" I said, pointing to the spot on the mattress.

I watched his face go pale. That made me even more nervous.

"It's okay," he said. "Don't be scared. Your mother will be home soon and she'll take care of everything." Then he went back into the kitchen.

I stood there not knowing what to do. *Why isn't Tatu calling the doctor?* I thought. *How does he know that I'll be all right?* My fear started to make me dizzy, so I sat down and put my head in my hands.

I stayed put until my mother came home. When she walked into the apartment, I could see from the bedroom that Tatu was whispering something in her ear. She came into the bedroom and after taking the sheets off the bed, she knelt down in front of me. I didn't know anything about girls getting their period until she explained it. I was so relieved to find out it was totally normal. And that it meant I was really growing up.

"You know, every young lady should have shoes with a little heel," Mama said. "I was about your age when I got my first pair. How about I take you shopping for them when we get to Munich?"

"Oh yes, that would be lovely," I said, throwing my arms around her neck for a hug.

9

Munich

THE YEAR WAS 1947. I was eager to get to Munich, but first we had to stop in Steyr, a beautiful Austrian mountain town. We ended up staying there for six weeks, and I came to love it. I met a girl named Halina, who had long, straight blond hair, which she let hang loose on either side of her face. We became fast friends. She and I walked arm in arm through the old cobbled streets, hitting on every topic of conversation we could think of. We had known each other for only a short time, yet it felt as if we had been friends forever. It's amazing how that can happen with some people you meet, as if your first conversation is more like picking up where you left off the last time you were together.

Steyr gave me a taste of normal life. A true best friend to confide in. The freedom to be carefree. I felt safe there. But before I knew it, we were packing *again* and I was saying a tearful good-bye to Halina and leaving for the big German city of Munich.

When I got my first sight of Munich, a chill ran down my spine and I raised my hand to my mouth, completely gobsmacked. The city had almost been obliterated. I had my face glued to the van's window as we passed blocks and blocks of destruction.

Munich had been ravaged in the war. It was where Hitler had first come to power, and after the war was over, the Allies took control of the city and the rest of Germany. Buildings were almost completely razed, with blocks of cement and other debris strewn across streets. Some only had the facades and frames of front windows intact. Yet the streetcars were running, and everyone went about their business as if nothing had happened.

Soon, we arrived at our new temporary home: an old barrack where soldiers had once slept. This was where the Jewish organization that was helping us immigrate to America was placing us and other Jewish families for the time being. I looked around at our accommodations with a sinking stomach. There were two long rows of beds with scratchy-looking wool blankets, a low ceiling with a single lightbulb hanging, and hardly any windows. It resembled a prison or a scary hospital. My eyes met my mother's. She grabbed my hand and gave it a squeeze.

We had no choice but to stay for the night. I didn't have any books to read, or a notebook to write in, so I decided to lie on my new narrow bed and make up stories in my head while staring at the ceiling. I thought about how much I missed Halina, my friend from Steyr, and Dora, my friend from Kraków. I also thought about Lala and missed her too. I thought about what life had been like back in Lvov, before the war and before everything changed. I felt so far from anyplace that seemed like home. A wave of tightness rose from the bottom of my neck up my throat, and when I squeezed my eyes shut, big, heavy teardrops slid down my cheeks.

The next morning, thankfully, Tatu went out to find us a better place to stay than the army barrack. He came across a room to sublet in an apartment belonging to a couple named Mr. and Mrs. Gelbart. They were also displaced persons—Holocaust survivors—and had been living in Munich for a while.

When we got to their apartment, I saw that the Gelbarts had rearranged the furniture for us so there would be space for three cots, and they set up a folding table with three chairs.

"Do you think Mrs. Gelbart would mind if I pushed my bed against the wall?" I asked my mother.

The three beds were arranged next to each other. "It'd be nice to have some privacy."

"I'm sure she wouldn't mind," my mother said. "I can ask her. *Or* I can ask her if she wouldn't mind if we brought in a rented piano for you to put there instead."

A piano! My heart leapt with happiness. I hadn't played piano in a while and missed it.

"Which do you think you'd prefer?" Mama asked me.

I decided to leave my cot where it was, of course.

I was grateful to the Gelbarts for letting us stay with them. And every day I was grateful to have my two parents, unlike so many other children who had survived the war. But I wasn't sure how long we'd be in Munich, or when we'd get to America. Life felt totally out of my control. Especially when my parents announced to me, a few days later, that I wouldn't get to attend school in Munich.

10

Stuck at Home

I FELT THE BLOOD rise to my cheeks when my parents told me I was going to be tutored at home.

"It's not fair," I told them, stomping my foot. I knew I sounded immature, but I couldn't help it. I slumped down in one of the dining chairs and crossed my arms. "Why won't you let me go to school? I'm an almost-teenager, and I'll have no life being holed up in this place! Don't you want me to make friends? Don't you want me to have a normal life already?"

"Luncia, I know it isn't easy for you to understand," Tatu said firmly. "But there's still a strong anti-Jewish sentiment in Munich, even though the Nazis were defeated and the Germans are no longer in control of the city. It might not be safe for you."

"But I'll be careful!" I cried. "I can take care of myself, you know. I'm not a little girl anymore!"

"No buts," Mama said. "The answer is no. And why are we even talking about this now? It's summertime, and you wouldn't start school until September."

I understood that my parents were probably right. Still, I didn't want to give in. I was sick of being isolated from the world.

My mother sat next to me at the table.

"I plan to keep my promise, you know, and get you shoes with a little heel," she said, leaning her head toward me and catching my gaze as I looked up from my lap. "Why don't I take you for them next week?"

I didn't want to smile. I didn't want to give her the satisfaction. But I felt the corners of my mouth turn up.

"And a new notebook. And a library card?" I threw in. There was no way she could refuse me.

"Yes and yes," she said, jokingly rolling her eyes.

As promised, my mother took me shopping the following week. I got new shoes with a small heel, a library card, and a hardcover notebook with lined pages. A journal, all for me. I decided to call the journal "My Little Mirror" so that one day in the future—hopefully in America—I could look at it to see what my life had been like in the past.

I don't know if it had anything to do with my new shoes or the journal, but I started to feel more grown-up. Not so much in the way I looked, but how I felt about myself. I was more confident and felt surer of my opinions and expressing them.

Another piece of happiness came in the mail. Our family in New York sent us packages, and they contained hand-me-down clothing from my cousins. Their dresses were long and came with matching short-sleeved fuzzy sweaters and cardigans. Most of my own dresses had sailor collars and bottoms with kick pleats. My cousins' clothes looked much more grown-up.

In the latest box was a long navy-blue skirt that tickled my ankles when I twirled around. I put it on with my new heeled shoes and imagined what my life would be like wearing a similar outfit when I lived in New York. As I stood admiring myself in the mirror, I overheard Mr. Gelbart telling my mother that through a miraculous coincidence, he found out that he had a cousin who had survived the Holocaust and was living in Munich.

"He's a young man who was liberated from Dachau," Mr. Gelbart explained. Dachau is the name of a town in Bavaria north of Munich and was also the name of a Nazi concentration camp.

"I ran into him in the street earlier today,"

Mr. Gelbart went on. "His name is Jack Gruener. He survived ten concentration camps, then learned his parents were killed. He's been struggling since the war ended, and he's such a nice boy. I told him he could come live with us."

11

Meeting Jack

I THREW A PILE of clothes onto the bed. I had almost given up.

"Where is the navy-blue skirt that Cousin Izzy sent?" I called to my mother from behind our bedroom door. "I *really* want to wear it today," I said.

"It's in a pile of things that need mending," my mother answered from the kitchen. "There's a hole in the seam."

I quickly threw on one of my older dresses with kick pleats in the skirt and ran into the kitchen.

"But I need the skirt *today*," I begged her. "It makes me look so grown-up."

The words were barely out of my mouth when Mama got a knowing look in her eyes. The mysterious Jack Gruener would be arriving that afternoon.

When Jack walked through the door, the first thing I noticed was that he didn't have anything with him except a small black hardcover notebook. Then I noticed how handsome he was, with wavy blond hair, brown eyes, and a winning smile.

Stop it stop it! I ordered myself, realizing I was fussing over creases in my skirt. I had a habit of repeatedly smoothing them out with my hands when I got nervous. *Why am I even nervous?* I asked myself. *It isn't like a matchmaker is introducing me to a suitor!*

Jack shook hands with his cousin Mr. Gelbart and greeted Mrs. Gelbart with a hug, thanking them both for taking him in. When Mrs. Gelbart introduced us, Jack offered a polite and gracious hello to my parents—and completely ignored me! He just gave me a quick glance and turned his attention back to the adults.

I almost wanted to jump in front of Jack and shove my hand in his face so he'd acknowledge my presence, but I had better manners than that.

He's being so rude! I thought. *Like I'm not worthy of being in his presence.*

Jack was only a few years older than I was, but I gathered that he saw me as a child. I glanced down at my knee-length, kick-pleat skirt and sighed. I decided to retreat to the bedroom to be alone. I sank into the chair in front of the dressing table thinking I'd write in my diary, but I just stared at myself in the mirror. My long hair was done up in two braids with bows tied at both ends.

Of course he thinks I'm a kid, I realized, sizing up my reflection and feeling frustrated. *There's nothing about me that looks grown-up, except for my new shoes. And what are the chances that he would notice my feet!*

I undid my braids, letting my wavy brown curls

fall to my shoulders, then shoved the ribbons into the bottom drawer of the bureau and slammed it shut. *That's it,* I swore to myself. *If my mother doesn't let me cut my babyish long hair already, I'll have a fit!*

For months, I had been asking her to let me wear my hair short in a more sophisticated style. Every time I asked, she said no. It felt like she always said no, no matter what. When I asked for a reason why, she told me it wasn't up for discussion—I hated that!—and I'd turn and storm away with my arms crossed.

The next afternoon, I was writing in my diary and my mother was in the kitchen. Suddenly, a new surge of frustration welled up in me. I had to do something—*something*—that made me feel like my life was moving forward in some way. That I was grown-up. That I wasn't stuck.

I took the scissors from the top drawer and went into the kitchen. My mother was fixing lunch. I held the scissors in front of me. Before I even opened my mouth, Mama swiped the scissors out of my hand, took my arm, and set me down in the dining chair. Before I knew it, I heard snipping right below my ears. My heart pounded as piles of hair fell to the floor around my feet.

At last she finished, and after dropping the scissors on the table, she spun me around in the chair to face her.

"Happy now?" From her intonation, I knew she really wasn't irritated, and so I gave her a kiss and ran back to the mirror. I looked so much older! Mama came and put one hand on my shoulder and with the other opened the drawer to put the scissors away.

"You're growing up, Luncia," she said with a smile. "It's a blessing, but never rush the time away. When you're young you don't realize how fast life passes, until one day you look back and don't know where the years went."

Going through something like war forces you to

grow up quickly whether you want to or not. Part of me understood what she said, except she didn't know what it was like to feel so behind in life—that I had missed out on the past and didn't feel any closer to my future.

12

Living in Limbo

ONE AFTERNOON IN 1947, I sat at the kitchen table with a stack of composition books, writing. My Polish writing skills were good, but I knew when we got to America, I'd have to start at an American high school. The thought filled me with anxiety.

What's going to become of me? I would ask myself in my most desperate moments. *There are so many gaps in my knowledge.* Passing my final high school exam and graduating seemed like a dream I doubted I would ever achieve. Catching up and learning

English at the same time didn't seem possible.

My anxiety would quickly switch to anger. *If it wasn't for Hitler, I would have attended middle school, I would have had friends, and I would have played the piano for nine years already!* I screamed in my head. *Instead I live like a hermit!*

To make matters worse, there was no news concerning our visas. Apparently, there were issues with the paperwork, and we weren't sure when—or if—the documents would come through.

I was tired of being so unsure about the future, and what the next day would bring. I didn't want to live like a vagabond without a permanent home. I knew hundreds of thousands of displaced people were experiencing the same thing. Countries around the world had quotas for the number of Jews they would allow to emigrate. And governments kept changing their rules. That meant more confusion and chaos—and more time in limbo.

Just then, Jack came into the kitchen to fix

himself lunch. I kept my eyes on my pencil moving across the paper.

"Can I get you anything, Luncia?" Jack asked.

I looked up, surprised he was actually addressing me. So far he had hardly said a word to me. *Maybe he's too embarrassed or shy to talk to me in front of my parents?* I thought.

"No, thank you," I answered politely. I self-consciously started to loop my finger through my newly cropped curls. I thought I might catch his gaze for a minute, but he just nodded and went back to what he was doing.

I knew he wouldn't notice, I thought, deflated. I had six inches of my hair chopped off and he wasn't look-ing at me any differently. And I was so sure I looked more mature!

I turned back to my composition book, still twirl-ing my hair.

Maybe he just sees through me, I considered. If I was honest with myself, my haircut may have made me look older, but I still felt stuck in childhood.

As time went on, Jack became close with my parents, and after a while, he finally began to acknowledge me more. I think he eventually realized that I wasn't some silly little kid, since I was always reading or writing in my notebook. Jack wrote too. He'd compose long poems that were quite good, and he'd read them aloud to us.

One night after dinner, he said that he had written a new poem and wanted to share it with us. He said it was about Aphrodite, the goddess of beauty, and shot me a look when he said it that made me blush.

While he stood in the living room reading the poem, I remained at the table, pretending to be engrossed in a book. After every few stanzas, out of the corner of my eye, I'd catch Jack glancing in my direction, and I'd blush all over again. I was sure my mother had noticed.

It wasn't too long after that night that Jack got his visa; he was going to board a ship bound for America. I wasn't sure how I felt about it—a mix of happiness for him and sadness for me.

The night before Jack left, he gave me the sheet music I had once mentioned to him that I was interested in learning.

"Here, Luncia," he said, handing me the sheet music. "I wanted to get you something that would make you happy. Hopefully, when you play these scores, you'll remember me and the time we spent together here at the Gelbarts'."

It isn't my birthday or anything, I thought as I took the papers from him and thanked him. I felt the color rise to my cheeks. *Why is he going out of his way to make sure I remember him?*

I was utterly clueless.

13

Good News and Bad News

JACK HAD LEFT FOR America, but my parents and I still had to wait—for almost another year. In early June 1948, we finally heard about the status of our visas—but it was very bad news. There was a strong possibility that we weren't going to be able to immigrate to America. I was so depressed. *Why are we to suffer so much?* I thought. *Have we not gone through enough already? Why is our fate being kicked around?* Our plans for the future got crushed in the blink of an eye. It was hard to stay positive after such a huge blow. *More waiting. More agonizing.* It was dreadfully tiresome.

But then, just as quickly as things had unraveled, they came together again. Tatu went back to the consulate the following week and found out that our papers were approved and our visas were getting processed! We'd be going to America.

Only eight days later, we found out that we would have to wait another year before emigrating to the United States. The Displaced Persons Act had been passed by Congress in 1948, and there were new quotas for who would be allowed to emigrate. It seemed that our luck had completely run out.

On that day, my parents sat at the table with their heads in their hands. I stood in the doorway, unsure if I should stay and listen to their conversation or go outside.

"I'll send a letter to our relatives in America to let them know," Tatu said, deflated.

"At least we're comfortable at the Gelbarts'," my

mother offered, doing her best to sound optimistic. "Maybe we'll hang a curtain so that Luncia has some privacy."

She looked at me as she said this, and I gave her an appreciative smile. As a teenager, sharing a room with one's parents was a real pain.

It was true that life wasn't horrible in Munich, but the German soil burned under our feet and we were anxious to leave for that reason too. Plus, for me, it meant another year of being homeschooled, which I didn't like at all.

Not that I had any real reason to believe it, but I thought by the time I was a teenager I'd be in America. On my fourteenth birthday, Mama bought me a beautiful baby-blue silk nightgown with a dot pattern, ribbons, and embroidery, and Tatu gave me a lovely pencil set. My mother's friend Genia got me a professional-looking manicure kit. The presents cheered me up and made me feel like maybe being a teenager here in Munich would be all right. And that fall, right before the Jewish New Year, my mother surprised me with my very first dressy hat. It was brown, and the perfect style for someone my age. Paired with my new long dress with a houndstooth pattern, I felt very grown-up.

The holiest day of the year for Jews is Yom Kippur—the Day of Atonement. Adults fast for an entire day to honor it, and I was able to do it for the first time. More evidence of my growing up! I stayed with my parents in synagogue all day, praying from early in the morning until it got dark. Going to synagogue in Munich, the city where Hitler came to power, gave us a little anxiety, but we also felt victorious for being able to openly practice Judaism.

Still, I couldn't help but dream of America, where, I hoped, we'd feel even freer.

❧

Later that fall, my parents signed up me up for piano lessons with a young man named Professor Wagner.

For the first lesson, he came to our apartment so he could meet Mama and Tatu, and he was a wonderful teacher.

The second lesson at his apartment didn't go as well.

I wore my new hat and dress that day. When I arrived at his door, his maid answered and invited me into the study, saying that Professor Wagner wasn't home yet but would be soon. I sat down on the piano bench and decided I might as well lift the cover and start to play.

"You're very talented and beautiful," Professor Wagner said a few minutes later, walking into the room. I swung around, and he came up close behind and handed me a piece of candy. "You'll go very far in the field of music if you trust me and listen to my instructions."

I'm sure I blushed at his words. I thanked him for the compliment and promised to be a good student.

Then came another compliment.

"You have lovely hands," he continued, taking mine in his. "Perfect pianist hands," he said, and raised one up to his eye level. "These long, elegant fingers . . ." Then he drew both of my hands to his lips to kiss them.

That made me nervous. I pulled my hands away and returned to playing. But as I tried to make sense of what had just happened, my hands started to shake.

"Oh, you poor thing," he said. "You must be cold. It's always a little chilly in this drafty old house. Give me your hands and I'll warm them in mine, and you'll play even better."

"No, thank you" was all I could manage to say.

Luckily, that was where it stopped. I was so upset about the whole thing, feeling so silly and inexperienced. I didn't know if it was decency and charm on his end or if it was something else. I was afraid to tell my mother, so I confessed everything to her friend Genia, who had become my confidante in all things grown-up.

"I didn't know what to do, Genia," I said. "Was he just being polite? I remember when Mrs. Gelbart's brother came, he kissed my hand the first time we met, but this felt different."

"What Professor Wagner did was improper," Genia said immediately. "It was completely out of line, and nothing excuses that kind of behavior—ever."

She made sure I heard her loud and clear. I nodded my head.

"You must always tell someone if anything like that ever happens again, with Professor Wagner or with anyone else," Genia continued.

I begged her not to say anything to my mother, because Professor Wagner was a good teacher and I didn't want to stop my lessons. In retrospect, though, I wish I had told my parents what had happened. But since I knew then what I was dealing with, I wanted to learn how to handle myself in those situations.

When Professor Wagner took my hand in his

during our next lesson, I immediately snapped it back and shot him an uncompromising look. He mumbled an apology, but I quickly cut him off and coolly asked about the exercise. I knew it wouldn't be the last time he would try something, and I would always need to keep my guard up.

As it turned out, I didn't have to.

By some miracle, the paperwork for our visas went through despite the new emigration quotas. We would leave for the German city of Bremen in three days to stay at a displaced persons camp before boarding our ship to America. To New York City.

I couldn't believe it was really happening. Finally, our luck held.

14

A New Year

MY PARENTS AND I packed up and moved from Munich to Camp Grohn, in a suburb of the city of Bremen. Camp Grohn had been a military base taken over by the United States Army after the war, and it housed more DPs awaiting emigration than any other camp in Germany.

The plan was that we would set sail for America on January 7, 1949, on the SS *Marine Flasher*. Starting in May 1946, the postwar immigrant ship would often bring hundreds of DPs—the vast majority of them Jews from all over Europe—to America from Germany each time it crossed the Atlantic Ocean. We were supposed to leave from Bremen, but at the very last minute, we found out that we would board the ship in the nearby city of Hamburg—and that the ship's final destination wasn't New York City. We were going to Boston, Massachusetts, instead!

We panicked. Even if we wrote to our family in America to let them know we weren't going to arrive in New York, they might not get the letter in time.

"I hope they find out somehow that the boat will dock in Boston, or they won't know what happened to us!" Tatu exclaimed.

"I'm sure there will be an announcement of some kind, maybe in the newspaper," my mother reasoned. "We can try to phone them when we get to Boston before getting on the train to New York."

That seemed like the best plan.

One week before we left Europe, on December 31,

1948, I attended my first-ever New Year's Eve party. Dances and other social events happened all the time at DP camps. Right after the war ended, the conditions at the camps were generally very poor, but they started to improve when the Allies took them over. Although it wasn't a *home*—we were all in transit there, on our way to someplace else—people were still able to live somewhat regular lives. There were neat brick row houses with white-paned windows and grassy fields with trees, where people played sports and kids had tons of space to run around. Children were born. Weddings and Jewish holiday celebrations took place.

My parents let me go to the New Year's Eve party alone, which was huge, considering they were still so overprotective. When I arrived at the party, I quickly found a group of people my age to dance with.

"My feet are killing me, but I don't care!" I yelled to the girl dancing the foxtrot with me.

"What? I can't hear you!" she yelled back over my shoulder. The band was playing loudly, and it was hard to hear.

"Never mind!" I said, then caught a glimpse of another new friend motioning over to the table with punch, signaling that we should take a break.

It wasn't everything I expected my first ball to be—I didn't have a date or a corsage on my wrist—but I was having a wonderful time.

I wiped the sweat from my forehead, took a sip of my punch, and looked around at the crowd. I'd felt so lost and impatient all these years in Europe, waiting to leave. But now that our trip to America was impending, I was nervous about leaving and wondered if everything I dreamed about was going to come true.

Lately, I'd noticed how much my parents had aged since we were liberated back in Lvov. They didn't move as quickly as they used to, and the lines on their faces were deeper. The traveling had taken a toll on them—perhaps even more so than it did on me. I hoped they would be able to weather the big journey.

The week flew by, and soon enough, my parents and I were on our way to Hamburg to board the ship. I was so overwhelmed by what was happening, I hardly knew what to do. It felt like a dream that I would have to wake up from soon. But it was real.

15

Good-Bye, Germany

PEOPLE FORMED TWO LONG lines on the dock while waiting to board the SS *Marine Flasher*. It was chaotic. Parents struggled to hold children's hands while bending down to inch their black suitcases forward. Young men traveling solo had duffel bags slung over their shoulders. Soldiers stood around to keep things organized, and the ship's crew members were busy on deck preparing for the boat's departure.

Oof. My stomach started doing flip-flops when I

thought about our journey ahead, which I knew wasn't going to be easy. I had heard stories about crossings that were treacherous, with waves that would come crashing down over the deck, one after another.

Be brave! I told myself. *You narrowly escaped death so many times during the Holocaust! A boat ride is nothing in comparison to what you've been through. The only alternative is staying in Germany. Would you rather have that?*

There was no turning back now.

At two thirty in the afternoon, my parents and I picked up our luggage and stepped onto the foot ramp. The boat's deck was packed with people, waiting for the moment when the ship's horns would blast to announce we were leaving the port. I was busy taking pictures with my camera, dragging Tatu all over so I could document everything on film while Mama stayed with our luggage. There was so much to see I didn't know where to aim first.

It took a long time for the passengers—a total of 549 displaced persons—to board. Finally, at around 4 p.m., the horn blew and I felt the boat's engine roar beneath my feet. We were off! Any anxiety I'd been feeling completely disappeared, replaced by exhilaration. Everyone was cheering and jumping up and down and hugging each other. My parents and I shared one long embrace and bent to touch our heads together.

"We did it," Tatu said. "Once we're settled in America, hopefully we'll look back on these long years of wandering and it'll seem like a blip in time."

We left the deck to find our sleeping quarters. Our room had four bunk beds neatly made with tucked-in blankets and sheets. There was no window, and I noticed two buckets on the floor in the corner. I didn't want to be in there for more than a minute so I could return to the decks with my camera.

When I got to the top deck, I watched the shoreline of Germany disappear as our ship made its way into the North Sea. Standing there, with my hair blowing in the breeze and my face to the wind, I felt like a character from a movie or romance novel.

The only difference was that scenes like that often happen at the end. But my story was just about to begin.

16

On Board

I WAS SO SLEEPY and full. I couldn't remember the last time I had eaten so much. The dining room on the ship had more than a dozen round tables lavishly set with china and floor-length white tablecloths. Silver trays held chicken, fruits, potatoes, and wonderful compotes (fruit stews), plus cookies, gingerbread, cakes, and other desserts for after our meal. It felt like we were guests invited to a fancy, formal affair. I was glad my mother suggested that I change into my nicer dress!

After we had eaten our fill, we all stumbled back to our cabin and headed to bed. I fell into a dream, but at 1:30 a.m., I was woken up by the boat rocking so hard I couldn't lie still in bed, bouncing from one side to the other. I gripped the metal frame to try to prevent getting tossed around, but I couldn't hold on and sleep at the same time.

I looked down at my parents on the two bottom bunks and saw that they were stirring too. The rocking seemed to be getting worse, because our belongings began sliding across the floor. Then the concert of vomiting started echoing through the halls. I did everything I could to avoid throwing up. I tried to persuade myself that I wasn't seasick, but I only made it till 6 a.m., when I joined the chorus.

Why, why, why did I have so much for dinner? I moaned to myself in agony. *Never again will I be able to look at the foods I ate!*

We had a respite from nonstop rocking for the

short time we made our way through the English Channel. After days of seasickness, it felt so good to be well. We started moving our watches back by one hour each day to get used to the time difference between Europe and America.

The lounge on the upper level had a small piano, called a pianoforte, and I spent time playing it in the afternoon with a group of passengers as my audience. I also had my accordion with me, which I had learned to play from one of my piano teachers while living in Munich, so I went out on deck to entertain everyone strolling in the sunshine. I also got to practice my English with a steward on the ship who spoke the language.

The worst part of our journey came at the end, the day before we were due to arrive in Boston. A storm started late in the afternoon while we were sitting in the lounge and the staff came in to shut the windows using airtight covers. The rocking was so intense that people just spilled out onto the floor left and right. We could hear dishes breaking in the dining room and the cries and screams of scared children. An urgent announcement ordered all passengers back to their cabins.

"I'm scared," I said to my parents, knowing that I sounded like a little kid.

"You have to have faith," Tatu said.

"Yes," Mama added. "You must believe in your heart that we are meant to be in America."

I nodded. That was all I could cling to. We had made it so far. There had to be a reason to make it.

At night, I lay down with my mother on her bed because she didn't want me to fall off the top bunk. I shivered and tried to sleep. I never would have expected that we would be so close to drowning when we were almost at shore.

17

America, Here We Come

THE ROCKING OF THE ship finally lulled me to sleep, and somehow I slept through the rest of the night. Late in the morning, I opened my eyes. Instead of waking up to the sound of vomiting, I woke up to cheering! I felt a flutter of hope in my chest.

Tatu, Mama, and I quickly got dressed and ran to the upper deck. Almost all the passengers were out there, pointing to the thin line of beige stretched across the horizon in the distance. Was it land? Was it Boston?

"Look, look!" I shouted to my parents. "Is that it? I can't see!" We were all shielding our eyes from the sun and squinting.

"I don't know," my mother said. "We've been looking at the ocean for so many days I can't tell what I'm looking at anymore."

Excited murmurs spread from group to group. Everyone turned to their neighbors to ask the same question and then went back to shuffling from side to side to see over other people's shoulders.

Then, at last, the announcement came: The ship's captain said that we were approaching land! We were supposed to arrive at 8 a.m. that day, but the ship had been delayed by the storm. I didn't care about the delay. We had finally made it!

Commotion grew on the deck as land came into focus, and we could make out buildings in Boston's skyline. I felt a surge of happiness, but at the same time, I was anxious about the unknown fate that awaited me. Meanwhile, the land was getting closer and closer. I was becoming more nervous by the minute, unable to live in the moment I had dreamed of for years.

I gripped the railing with both hands as the *Marine Flasher* pulled into Boston Harbor. I forced myself to clear my head so I would be present when we docked. I knew that it would be something I would want to remember in the future, to tell my children and grandchildren what it felt like to be an immigrant first arriving in this country.

Journalists packed into small boats lined up along the *Marine Flasher*'s side. They held their big cameras up and waved so we would all wave back. Ours was the first ship of DPs to arrive in that year, so there were a lot of festivities planned to mark the occasion. American flags and red, white, and blue banners decorated the harbor's port, and a military band played patriotic songs, including "The Star-Spangled Banner," which I heard for the first time. The journalists kept snapping photos. With all the attention from the press, I felt a bit like a movie star, just like I had while watching Europe fade into the distance weeks before.

The sky was overcast and dreary, and it was brutally cold outside. My parents and I went to get our luggage from our cabin and brought it back onto the deck. Then Mama and I left Tatu to watch our bags while we went to collect our visas at the ship's canteen, which had been turned into a temporary office. After rejoining Tatu, the three of us disembarked. I was too busy looking at all the activity on the dock to notice that at last I was stepping onto American soil.

Next, my parents and I had to go through customs to have our visas checked and our bags inspected. I held my visa, running my finger along the edge. It was astonishing to think that the tiny piece of paper in my hand was the most important thing in the world. I looked younger in the photo on my visa. My cheekbones weren't as defined, and my eyes seemed wider. Still, the customs official seemed to acknowledge it was me—my visa got stamped, and we were officially allowed into the country.

To welcome the arrival of the ship, the mayor of Boston delivered a speech at the dock. He spoke in English, of course.

"What is the mayor saying?" Tatu whispered to me. "Can you understand?"

My mother turned her head to hear my answer.

"A few words here and there," I answered glumly, "but that's it. Not enough to translate for you."

Tatu put his arm around me and gave a squeeze.

"You're a very intelligent young woman, Luncia," he said. "You just wait. You'll be chattering away in English in no time."

"I hope so," I said, feeling my nervousness coming back.

At about 4 p.m., along with a crowd of other DPs, my parents and I boarded a train bound for New York City. It wasn't until we got on the train that I realized how cold I was from standing outside all day. My feet were so freezing they felt numb.

And in that instant, I was struck by a vivid memory. I flashed back to being in hiding at the Szczygiels' apartment.

The condensation of my breath clouded in puffs in front of me. From my burgundy settee, I eyed the ceramic stove in the corner with longing, wishing the stove would magically heat up and my body would thaw—especially my hands and feet, which were so cold they stung and itched. But Mrs. Szczygiel liked to save money, and she wouldn't turn the heat on until we went to bed. I tried pressing my hands underneath my armpits to get my blood flowing and crossing my legs beneath me to tuck my toes in the backs of my knees, but nothing helped. Babcia came in and told me to stop fidgeting so much or I'd make myself hungry. That's when I showed her my hands.

"My god, Luncia!" she nearly yelled. "Your hands are as red as beets! Take off your socks and let me see your feet." So I pulled off my socks, and when she saw

my red, swollen feet, she gasped and said, "You have
frostbite!"

I watched in terror as Babcia ran out of the room and
came back a few minutes later with a basin filled with
soggy potato peels. "Here," she said. "Soak your feet and
then your hands and the swelling will go down."
Thankfully, Babcia's solution helped, but I was scared
the frostbite would come back.

The train whistle blew and snapped me back to
reality. I shook my head. The memory had felt so
close. I realized that I hadn't thought about the
details of my life during the Holocaust very much
since the war ended. I'd been so focused on catching
up on schoolwork, and adjusting to each new place
we went to, and dreaming of America.

Why am I thinking about this now? I asked
myself. *Why on my very first day in this country?* I
let myself feel sad for a moment, then banished
the thoughts from my mind as the train pulled
forward.

Yes, Luncia, I told myself as the train sped up. *Forward. Only forward. Never back.*

That's what we, as Holocaust survivors, told ourselves when we came to America. It's what we told each other, at first. As time passed, we would come to realize that burying our memories would be much worse than remembering them.

18

Welcome to New York

I NEARLY TRIPPED ON the platform after we got off the train because I was walking with my eyes half-closed. The pungent smell of diesel filled my nose, along with the stench of cigarette smoke and sweat that was coming from the crowds around me. We had arrived at Grand Central Terminal in New York City.

Groggy and travel-weary, Mama, Tatu, and I dropped our bags in the station's cavernous main concourse. Looking up, my heart skipped a beat.

There was the sweeping, celestial mural on the ceiling. Straight ahead, a shiny, golden, four-faced opal-glass clock sat atop the information booth in the center of the hall. I had seen images of Grand Central Terminal once in a newsreel, when men were first coming home after the war. It looked in real life just as it had on the screen.

"Barbara, do you see them?" Tatu asked my mother. She was standing on her tiptoes with a photo of our relatives in hand, searching the crowd.

"Not yet," she answered. "There are so many people!"

Despite the late hour, commuters rushed past in a dizzying blur, darting around the people who were waiting to greet family. Reporters scurried about, talking to DPs and taking their pictures. Children in Polish national costumes danced in circles to Polish music, giving us a welcome performance. Volunteers from the American Red

Cross handed out coffee and cookies. The brouhaha of the unlikely scene barely fazed the commuters, who gave us little more than a glance. Most didn't even look over as they went about their business.

"Welcome to New York," I whispered to myself under my breath with a smile.

Then Tatu spotted his nephew Leon and Leon's young wife. They weren't holding a sign with our name—they held photos of us we had sent! They rushed over to us. We had never met, but I greeted them warmly in English, though I had difficulty calling to mind words I was sure I knew, because I was exhausted.

"This is my father, Isaac, and my mother, Barbara," I said clearly. Cousin Leon and his wife nodded hello. They were a handsome couple. He was tall and wore a sports coat with a carnation in the lapel. His wife was a brunette, with her hair pulled back into a high ponytail and bangs.

She was wearing a skirt with a felt poodle sewn on front, which was all the rage in fashion that year.

My parents spoke over each other to me in Yiddish, fighting to relay everything they wanted to say. I tried to interrupt them so I could continue translating. But they just kept going, so I eventually gave up.

Finally, they each took a breath. I turned to my cousin and his wife, offering what must have been a hilariously short sentiment after my parents' two-plus minutes of nonstop talking.

"They said it's nice to meet you too."

We carried our luggage out to the curb while Cousin Leon went to get his car. The buildings in New York City were so tall I had to crane my neck back to see the tops. I spun around on my heels to catch sight of the dazzling Chrysler Building looming above us.

We all piled into the car and drove to Queens, where Tatu's sister, Rebecca, and her husband,

Benny, lived. It wasn't far from Manhattan, and through the back-seat window I watched us leave the skyscrapers behind for tree-lined blocks with wide front yards and single-family homes.

Even though it was the middle of the night when we pulled up to the house, Aunt Rebecca and Uncle Benny came flying out the front door with open arms and quickly ushered us inside. Aunt Rebecca was beautiful, with curly dark hair. It was bittersweet to see Tatu embrace his sister, whom he hadn't seen in ages. Uncle Benny was thin with graying hair, and he looked like a university professor, even though he was a tailor.

My aunt and uncle's house was warm and cozy, and we gathered in the kitchen to talk a while longer before going to bed. Everything looked so new! The appliances were pink-and-mint-green enamel, with gleaming chrome details. Aunt Rebecca insisted on making tea and putting out snacks despite our protests for her not to fuss.

Cousin Leon was standing in the corner with his wife, who had her head inside the icebox. It sounded like they were having a tiff. I couldn't pick up the entire conversation—not because I didn't understand, but because it was difficult to hear. Then Cousin Leon's voice got louder.

"I told you in the station that you're wrong," he said. "And if you ask, you'll sound ridiculous—or worse, insulting! It isn't like they lived in the Dark Ages in Europe!"

"I was just trying to be nice," she pouted.

"What's this?" Aunt Rebecca asked, turning her head around to look at the couple.

Cousin Leon rolled his eyes. "Ma. You tell her that of course Luncia has had ice cream. She thinks she hasn't, and wanted to surprise her with a welcome treat to celebrate."

His wife crossed her arms and pouted again.

"Oh yeah?" she said. "Well, I bet she's never had an egg cream soda. She's never been to Brooklyn!"

Their eyes all fell on me.

"I've had ice cream before," I said, wanting to laugh. Of course I'd had ice cream! My parents had *made* ice cream at their chocolate shop, back in Lvov before the war.

Uncle Benny got up from the table.

"We should let them go to bed," he said. "I'll go make up the spare room."

19

That Place Called Brooklyn

I THOUGHT WAKING UP on my first day in America would feel momentous. It didn't.

I rolled over toward the window to look outside. There was an overcast gray sky. Bare tree branches caught in gusts of wind whooshed and rattled against the side of the house. It could have easily been a winter morning in Germany or Poland.

Why am I not more excited? I questioned myself as I lay there staring at the ceiling. *I've been waiting to start this life for years!*

I had gotten everything I wanted—the chance to have a permanent home, to start school, and make friends! Yet I felt detached and indifferent, like it was happening to someone other than me.

Maybe something is stopping you from enjoying it. The thought lingered in my mind. *Maybe you don't trust that it won't be taken away.*

I threw the covers off myself and stood up, putting my hands on my hips.

Or maybe you're just exhausted and should stop your maybe-ing!

After finding the bathroom, I lumbered down the steps to the kitchen. Everyone sitting at the table was already dressed.

"Good morning, Sleeping Beauty," my mother said. "Or should I say, good almost-afternoon?"

According to the clock above the stove it was nearly 11 a.m.

"So much for winding my watch back to get used to the time difference," I said with a yawn.

I ran upstairs to get dressed and the doorbell rang. Tatu's older brother, Abe, and his wife, Ida, had come over, and I heard them talking to my parents in the kitchen. When I went down, Aunt Rebecca was reading in the living room and told me to help myself to breakfast. As I cut slices of bread at the counter, I eavesdropped on the conversation. Tatu told Uncle Abe and Aunt Ida that he and my mother wanted to rent a storefront with an apartment in the back, so they could open a candy shop. Uncle Abe said that he had found my parents a furnished room in Brooklyn.

"It'll be good for now while you look for a better place," Uncle Abe said. He had kind eyes like Tatu, and he wore pleated trousers and shiny loafers. "In the meantime, why don't you let us take Luncia?" Uncle Abe offered, and I froze. "David is off at college, so we have a spare bedroom. James Madison High School is within walking distance of our house. Ida can get Luncia registered so she can start school.

And Ida can help Luncia with her English in the evenings."

It's a miracle I didn't cut off my finger slicing the bread. At Uncle Abe's words, the knife slipped out of my hand, skittered across the counter, and landed on the kitchen floor. It got everyone's attention.

"Isn't anyone going to ask me how I feel about this?" I protested when everyone turned to look at me. "Don't I get a say? Or am I supposed to sit back and let everyone plan what happens in my life?"

"Luncia! You're being rude," my mother snapped. "Uncle Abe is generously offering to give you room and board in their house so you'll have a comfortable place to get acclimated to life here and start your studies."

I dug my nails into the sleeve of my sweater to temper my anger and frustration.

"I'm sorry," I said, trying my best to sound believable.

Then I turned to Tatu and Mama.

"I can't imagine us being separated after all we've

been through," I said in a measured voice. I mentally complimented myself for keeping my emotions in check and not breaking down.

But my lips started quivering and I couldn't hold on anymore.

"I don't want to live in a different place than you!" I blubbered. "It'll be just like when I lived at the Szczygiels'!"

"It will not be just like living at the Szczygiels'," Tatu said, a little cross. "Uncle Abe and Aunt Ida are your real family, and we aren't hiding from the Nazis anymore!"

"Go upstairs and take your breakfast with you," my mother said. "Tatu and I will come up in a little while to talk with you about this."

❦

Later that afternoon, my parents tried to convince me that moving in with my aunt and uncle was the best thing to do.

"We won't really be apart," Tatu said. "Certainly not like we once were, during the war."

"Their apartment is only a half hour away by bus," my mother continued. "Besides, you'll be so busy with school that you won't even have time to miss us."

Oh. School. It hadn't hit me until my mother said it. I must have blocked it out when my aunt and uncle mentioned it because I was preoccupied with the living arrangement.

I'd waited so long for this time to come. School had been all I could think about after the war ended. And there I was, nervous—and dreading it.

20

The New American Me

I SAT ON THE front steps of Uncle Abe and Aunt Ida's house with my diary in my lap. It was windy and humid, an unusually warm day for January. The weather made my hair frizzy, causing me to fuss with the barrette I had fastened on the side to keep it in place. I looked up at the cloudless azure sky and slowly exhaled.

I was living in a neighborhood in Brooklyn called Midwood. Two weeks after stepping off the train at Grand Central, I was about to start James Madison

High School with my new, Americanized name: Ruth Gamzer.

Ruth? I'd thought to myself as my aunt Ida filled out my paperwork in the school's office a few days prior. *It's so different from Luncia.* I wasn't sure how I felt about it. My cousin Nettie had picked the name for me when we were taking a walk one Saturday afternoon. I didn't even have a chance to ask her why she picked it—she just said "You should call yourself Ruth now" with such certainty that I accepted it. After all, my cousin was American, and she must have known best about American names. So that was how I became Ruth.

I felt like I needed all the American-ness I could get. I was the only student at James Madison who had come from Europe. That first day, I headed off to school with a deep nervousness in my belly. I was sure I'd have no friends and would have to sit by myself at lunch.

But, somehow, the opposite happened: Being

unique made me popular! I suppose many of the kids were curious about the new girl who had come all the way from Europe and had survived the Holocaust. The teachers were extra kind to me, particularly my biology teacher, who told me I could copy notes from the other girls in the class to improve my English.

And somehow I found myself with a group of friends: Louise, Merna, Susan, and Norma. The girls linked arms with me on the way to class, and they got me up to date on all the latest news about who was going steady with whom. They gave me advice on everything. They shared secrets that only someone who went to James Madison for a long time would know. Every day, they would pick me up before school and walk me home in the afternoon.

Aunt Ida was an elementary school teacher. She came home earlier than I did a few times during my first two weeks so I wouldn't be in an empty house by myself. She must have seen everyone waving good-bye to me before I came inside.

"Well, aren't you popular," she said to me teasingly. "It's so nice you already have so many friends! I'm calling your mother right now to tell her. It'll make her very happy to hear that you're doing so well."

I was doing well—sort of. Aside from having a headache from eight hours of nonstop English, school was all right. But living with my aunt and uncle had its challenges. They did well financially—Uncle Abe was a chiropractor and Aunt Ida made a good salary as a teacher—so money wasn't tight and their lives were comfortable. My uncle was very generous. He saw that I only had two nice dresses for school that I swapped out every other day, so he treated me to a few new tops and skirts, which was very kind of him.

But Aunt Ida was the opposite, and stingy with food. I wasn't sure why. When my uncle prepared supper and put food on my plate, often my aunt would say, "That's too much for her," and remove half my food. I could feel her eyes on me at dinner. I didn't ever dare go into the refrigerator or pantry for fear that she would notice something missing and yell at me.

Every morning before work, my uncle made me lunch to take to school. Without knowing that my aunt had bought a bag of apples to cook with, he threw one apple in my lunch bag for a few days in a row. When my aunt realized the apples were gone, she automatically accused me of taking them!

"I didn't, I swear!" I said to her when she confronted me. "Uncle Abe put them in my lunch bag. Ask him when he gets home!"

She never apologized.

Because I'd been so seasick on the boat to America, I was thinner than I should have been. I got even skinnier at my aunt and uncle's. I would lie awake at night with my stomach growling so loudly that it kept me awake. I was hungry all the time, and I knew that feeling very well from when I was in hiding during the war. I would try to convince myself that I had just eaten a big meal so I would fall asleep, but it never worked. *I ate better on the* Marine Flasher*!* I thought with a sigh.

One morning, I was feeling a little better and getting ready in the bathroom before school. I looked around at the bathroom, and suddenly, I felt my legs and arms start to tingle. My mind raced as another vivid memory took hold, like it had the day we arrived in America. I remembered a time, while I was in hiding at the Oyaks', when I'd had to use the bathroom—but couldn't.

Back then, Mr. Oyak had found out that his mother had asked to spend the night at their house with a German friend for Christmas Eve. Mr. Oyak's mother had no idea that he and his wife were hiding three Jews in their home, but Mr. Oyak knew he couldn't say no to his mother's visit, or she would become suspicious. The solution was to hide us— my father would hide inside the porthole built above the bathtub. And my mother and I would hide inside the bottom half of a credenza in the common room.

The inside of the credenza was tiny and dark. I stared at it, terrified, remembering the nightmare of my "coffin" back at the Szczygiels'. I began to tremble. How would I survive in there, even for one night?

I watched as my mother lined the bottom with clean rags, and she climbed inside first. I climbed in after her, scrunching up tight. The space was small and stifling.

"Luncia," Mama whispered. "Feel for a nail sticking out at the top of the inside of the cabinet door. Do you feel it?"

"I think so," I said, straining. "I can barely reach it though."

"Well," she continued, "you're going to have to grab on to it to shut the door closed. So stretch!"

I did as she told me, and then we sat there together in the darkness. I was scared and anxious and, worst of all, I realized I had to go to the bathroom. But I knew it was too late to climb out of our hiding spot—the guests were here. I heard glasses clinking and people singing Christmas carols. I tried pretending that I was at the party too, in a pretty dress running around and playing with the other children, but I couldn't keep my mind off my problem.

"Mama," I whispered. "I'm sorry, but I have to go. What am I going to do?"

"Why do you think I put all these rags in here?" she said. "Do what you have to do."

As uncomfortable as it was, I had no choice, and then my mother pushed the soiled rags into the far corner of the credenza with her foot and told me to try to go to sleep. Eventually, I did.

A car horn blared outside and startled me. I glanced at the clock near the bed and realized I was going to be late.

As usual, my friends had come to pick me up for our walk to school. It was almost the weekend, when the thing to do in nice weather was to stroll along Emmons Avenue and look at all the boats docked along the piers. As we headed to school, the girls talked about their weekend plans, and about the Winter Dance. Everyone was very excited about what they planned to wear and which boys they wanted to go with. I half listened and smiled every so often so they'd think I was paying attention. My English had gotten good enough that I could follow along in all conversations.

But I couldn't shake off the feeling that stuck with me from what I had remembered of my time in hiding.

What's happening to me? I wondered. *Why am I feeling these things now when I'm safe in America and the war is over?* I didn't understand. *You're supposed to be happy now, living a happy life!* I reminded myself. *You're living your dream! Why can't you just forget everything and move on?*

It seemed that the more I told myself to forget, the more all the memories came rushing back.

21

A Lesson in Fun

ONE AFTERNOON, MY GROUP of friends asked me to meet them by the school's office after the last bell.

I got all the books I'd need for homework out of my locker and walked to the office to meet them.

"Ruth, we want you in our club," Louise said. "But you have to go through an initiation first before you can join."

They debated over something ridiculous to make me do. Wear my dress inside out. No, that was too mean, they decided. Finally, they came up with it.

"You have to wear two different color socks to school every day for a week," Louise declared.

This all seemed strange to me. But I was beginning to realize that teenagers in America liked to have something called "fun." "Fun" was a concept I didn't understand. In Europe, life had been so much about survival. The idea of "fun" seemed trivial, and a little childish. Yes, I enjoyed things like spending time with my friends, or going to the library and reading a good book. But wasn't "fun" what babies had when they played together? I wasn't sure.

But I did know that I wanted to belong. So on Monday, I went to school wearing two different socks. No one said anything except one of my teachers, who pulled me aside in the hall after class. She was trying to be kind to let me know the mistake I had made, until I told her I did it on purpose. I waited for her to scold me. Instead, she smiled.

"Oh, Ruth!" she said. "That's wonderful! Just look at you! You haven't even been here a month yet and you're already becoming an American teenager."

I didn't know how to take that. On one hand, I was happy because I felt included—which was all I'd wanted. But I knew, deep down, I was different from my friends. Everyone was very nice, and I was grateful to have a group of friends. But none of them understood what I had been through, and I didn't feel comfortable talking about my experiences with them. I couldn't really relate to them or my other classmates on anything deeper than the surface. That made me feel like something was missing.

Perhaps I'm *the one who's missing something,* I thought later that week, as I got home from school. I should have been gleeful, because I'd now formally been accepted into the "club." But I kept wondering how different I would be if I hadn't gone through the war and the Holocaust. *I'm so serious all the time. If I were as happy-go-lucky as my American friends are, I bet I'd fit in a lot better.*

The thought made me angry—angry at everything

152

I had been forced to suffer through and, at that moment, angry at the fact that I still didn't feel as grown-up as I wanted to, or as settled, or as happy as I had expected I would be. That too-familiar anxiety I had moving from place to place in Europe flashed through me like wildfire.

It also didn't help matters that I missed my parents terribly. My mother visited as often as she could, but no matter how long she stayed, I wished it were longer. She noticed I was getting thin, so she would pack a sandwich and stash it in her purse to bring me. I'd hide it in the top drawer of the desk in my room and eat half after dinner before bed and the other half the next morning as a second breakfast before school.

One Sunday, Mama came to see me with interesting news.

"Your father got a letter from Jack," she told me, and my ears perked up. Jack Gruener, from Munich!

"What did Jack say?" I asked.

153

"After only a short time in America, he's been sent to fight the war in Korea," Mama said, shaking her head. "The poor young man has had enough war to deal with!"

"That's so unfair," I said. I felt a twinge of worry, thinking of Jack going off to fight in a war. "He hasn't even been an American citizen for very long."

"You should find time to write to him," my mother said. "I'm sure getting a letter from you would really boost his spirits."

From then on, I promised myself that I would write Jack at least one letter a week no matter how much homework or studying I had to do. It wasn't just because my mother said I should either. I liked Jack, though I wasn't sure if I liked him as a friend or something more.

❧

Even though keeping up with school wiped me out, I decided to get part-time work to help my parents as much as I could. Considering that my English was only so-so, it wouldn't be easy to convince someone to hire me. But I went from store to store asking to speak to the manager until I found a job. The job was at Woolworth, which was a huge department store chain. Woolworth stores were also called "five-and-dimes" because when the store first opened in the late 19th century, everything cost either five or ten cents.

I worked at the Woolworth four days a week after school, and also on Saturday nights, which definitely curtailed many of my opportunities for "fun." Lots of kids had jobs after school, but my aunt and uncle lived in a well-to-do neighborhood, so many of the kids used what they earned for play money. I worked to save for basic things I needed.

"How come you don't get ice cream after lunch, Ruth?" Norma asked me one day while we were at recess.

I was embarrassed to admit to her that even though

I worked, I didn't have extra money.

"I don't really like ice cream," I said, lying because I didn't know what else to do.

"Who doesn't like ice cream?" Merna jumped in, laughing. "You don't even buy soda! Don't tell me you don't like Coke!"

I shook my head.

"I don't like the bubbles," I lied again. "I hiccup and they go up my nose."

I also got a second job babysitting, which was a disaster because I had no idea how to take care of babies. My uncle had a patient who needed a sitter. He drove me to their house, and when we arrived there was an 18-month-old boy standing in the hall, and his mother held a tiny, five-month-old in her arms.

The couple put their children to bed before they left for the evening and told me not to pick up the infant from the crib. When they left, I settled down on the couch and thought about how cute the toddler was and how sweet the baby had looked in the mother's arms.

And then it came lightning fast—another horrific memory from the Holocaust. It was starting to happen very often, always without warning.

Tatu came back looking stricken. We were still living in our own apartment in Lvov before we moved to the ghetto, and my father heard that people were buying fake birth certificates to prove they were Christian. There was a couple selling them in our neighborhood, so he went to find out if he could buy them for us. He told us a Jewish family with a one-year-old boy was also at the apartment to get documents. The baby started to cry, so the mother picked him up, and suddenly a Nazi came charging through the door, grabbed the child out of the mother's arms, and dropped him out the window. The parents started wailing and everyone thought they would all be taken away, but the Nazi just walked back out.

"There's no sense to it," Tatu said to me and Mama. "There's no rhyme or reason for who gets killed and who

doesn't. It happens at their whim, whenever the urge strikes them to be monsters."

I was shot back to the present by the baby screaming in his crib. The screams woke up the toddler, who also started to cry when he realized his parents weren't home. With both kids hysterical, I sang, clapped, and even danced for them, but they wouldn't stop crying. Finally, I called my uncle—I was nearly in tears too at that point—and begged him to come back. He stayed with me until the parents got home. That was my first and last time babysitting.

❧

I thought about telling my mother and Tatu about my flashbacks, but I didn't want to get them worried. They had enough to think about, trying to find a way to get us on our feet without having to rely on the generosity of our relatives.

And it seemed that many people didn't want to hear our memories. When my parents and I were still staying with Uncle Benny and Aunt Rebecca back in Queens, Tatu started to tell them about what had happened to Uncle Hirsch and Aunt Clara and my grandmother, how they were taken from the ghettto and killed.

"We don't need to hear that now," Uncle Benny said before my father got very far with the story. "It's too sad to talk about."

In a way, I understood Uncle Benny. *You need to make the decision to stop all this nonsense,* I told myself. *Like kicking a bad habit. No one is going to want to be friends with a morose girl who can't talk about the Winter Dance because she's having flashbacks of herself with frostbite or thinking about a baby getting thrown out a window by a Nazi.*

Sometimes I wished that I'd get amnesia so my memories would be wiped out without a trace. I was tired of fighting. I was drowning in the storm that raged inside me.

22

Lonely No More

"GO AHEAD, OPEN IT," my cousin David said to me.

I flipped open the gilded hardcover of the German-English dictionary he made me as a welcome gift and found a note written in script on the title page:

To my very smart cousin Ruth, who speaks
more languages than anyone else I know.
Fondly yours, Cousin David

I gave him a big hug and thanked him, touched by his thoughtfulness. He was home from college for summer break. He was hoping to get a job as a life-guard at the beach or pool club.

"Oh, by the way," he said, pointing to the diction-ary. "I put all the slang words in there that you'll need to know. Not the really bad ones, of course," he said with a wink.

"I think I need to learn all the regular words first," I said with a laugh. Then I thought about the progress I needed to make in English before my junior year.

"I'm so embarrassed that I have to go to summer school," I said to David glumly. "It's the only way that I'll graduate on time."

"You shouldn't be embarrassed," he said in an upbeat voice. "Plenty of kids have to go to summer school at some point over four years of high school. I did for freshman algebra, and look at me now. An engineering major!"

David was like the older brother I never had. He let me keep his room and slept on the couch for the whole summer. I still desperately missed my parents, but having him around cheered me up immensely. When he wasn't hanging out with his friends, he'd take me to Coney Island and buy me crinkle-cut french fries from Nathan's and cotton candy. Then we'd go to Steeplechase Park to go on the famous Parachute Jump, called "Brooklyn's Eiffel Tower," and to Luna Park to ride the Cyclone.

There was a week in July when it didn't stop raining. David didn't get called into work at the pool club, and one afternoon I arrived home from summer school soaking wet, books and all. I had forgotten my umbrella and didn't have enough change for the bus.

David was on the couch when I walked in, and he started laughing when he saw me. I slammed my books on the counter and took off my shoes, totally annoyed.

"Aww, I'm sorry," he said, still laughing a little. "You should have called. I would have come to pick you up in the car."

I rolled my eyes at him and tossed my hands in the air.

"Hey, you know what?" he added a moment later. "I'm starved. I'm taking you for pizza at Totonno's."

I had heard about pizza but hadn't tried it yet. There were a lot of delicious new things to eat in Brooklyn. I figured I'd get to it eventually.

"You *have* had pizza, haven't you?" David asked.

"Nope," I said matter-of-factly. That was the great thing about having cousins in New York to hang out with. They helped me learn the kinds of things I wouldn't in school, and I never felt like an idiot in front of them for not knowing something.

"Pizza is a rite of passage," David said, grabbing the car keys. "And Totonno's Pizzeria Napolitana on Neptune Avenue is an institution."

David was right. Totonno's did not disappoint. Pizza was absolutely delicious, and I couldn't wait to have it again.

I had been living in America for six months and

had started to see my life a little differently by the end of that summer. Things weren't perfect—my parents hadn't found a way to start a business, they weren't financially independent, and they insisted that I still stay with my aunt and uncle. Yet I stopped looking for perfection in myself, and in my situation.

I realized that I had been holding on to the feelings of that scared little girl in hiding. I spent a lot of mental energy being afraid that something or someone was going to take away the new life I was building. That scared girl would always be a part of my past. But there's a difference between remembering something tragic that happened and talking about that memory, and constantly reliving it. I wouldn't forget, but I was learning how to make peace. The flashbacks I was having slowly became less frequent, and they didn't have the power over me that I once allowed them to.

I also came to terms with realizing that America

was never going to live up to the dream I had created. When the war ended, I'd just wanted to feel safe. Then I just wanted a normal life. But now I understood that normal life in America didn't mean that I would be on cloud nine all the time, always happy, always excited, and never sad or lonely. That wasn't reality. There would be ups and downs, with schoolwork, with friendships, and with all the things that make up the day-to-day. I'd still get caught in the rain, not always get perfect grades on every test, and have tiffs with my family every so often. That was life—real, normal life—whether I was living in Poland, or Germany, or Brooklyn.

23

Finding Home

I LAY IN BED, looking out David's bedroom window. The leaves on the trees were still mostly green, but a few were already starting to turn yellow-orange. Autumn was on its way.

David went back to college at the end of August. Not having him around to take me places or to help me with my homework or to watch TV made me feel really down. I hadn't felt like doing much more than read books as an escape.

I had lived with Uncle Abe and Aunt Ida for eight

months. Every time I saw my parents, I begged them to let me move in with them.

"I'm never going to feel truly settled until I live with you," I said for what seemed like the millionth time. "I have friends and I like them just fine, though they aren't true best friends. It's hard to get close to them, knowing that I'll likely be leaving some time before graduation."

Finally, my parents agreed. The prospect of restarting their business was coming together. In a Brooklyn neighborhood called East New York, they found a storefront with a basic apartment in back. They needed furniture and supplies for the store, so my aunts and uncles pitched in and helped out. Soon after, Barbara's Chocolates—named for my mother— opened its doors.

Going back to the way we lived during and after the war was oddly comforting, probably because it felt familiar. Like when we were at the Oyaks', I slept on a dining table that my mother made up with blankets.

But lying there one night after my parents went to sleep, I remembered the night I spent alone in my father's office after I escaped the ghetto. The terror of that experience started to claw its way into my mind.

No! I told myself, shaking myself awake. *I can think about it, and I can tell someone the story if I want of how I survived, but I won't let it take over and control me.*

I didn't have to sleep on the table for long. A few weeks later, a three-room apartment became available across the street from the store. It wasn't large, but it had a certain warmth to it. I had my own room— finally! My cousin Helen gave me her old dressing table, with three drawers on each side and a mirror. I would sit on its little bench with the crocheted seat and write in my diary every night before bed.

I also wrote to Jack almost every week. He was still in Korea, and he would send me letters regularly that I looked forward to receiving when I got home from school. He would always include a poem, confessing his love and longing to see me. I didn't understand where all his emotions came from since we hadn't seen each other in so long, but I did care very much for him. My mother had taken me for professional photos, and I sent one to Jack in a letter. He wrote back something that made me speechless; he said that I looked beautiful and that he couldn't wish for a better wife for himself, or for better in-laws than my parents. My face burned as I read the letter. I didn't know if he was proposing or if he was just giving compliments. I would have to wait and see.

Even though I was now living with my parents in East New York, I still had to finish out the term at James Madison High School. This meant I had to take two long bus rides to get to and from school every day. But it was worth it to be able to live with my parents again.

And then, after the new year, I started the second half of my junior year at my new school: Thomas

Jefferson High School. To my surprise, many of the students there were like me—they had emigrated from Europe after World War II and several of them were also Holocaust survivors. We had much more in common than I'd had with my classmates back at James Madison, so I felt a stronger connection to the kids at my new school right away.

Here, I found another group of friends, but our friendship felt deeper and truer. Fay, Birdie, Anne, and I would sit side by side at the luncheonette counter, drinking egg cream sodas every day after school. The four of us would walk up and down Pitkin Avenue and look in the windows of shops and the Simon Ackerman department store. On the weekends, especially once summer came around, we liked to go to Prospect Park or to the beach at Coney Island. We would see movies at Loew's Pitkin Theater and the Roxy. On special occasions, we would go into Manhattan to see a show at Radio City Music Hall. But our favorite place to hang out was at

Bay 5. It was the name of a street in Brighton Beach, and everyone would stand around at the spot just below the elevated train platform to check out the scene. At night, we would go to parties and dances in big ballrooms or someone's basement. There were a few boys who wanted to date me and go steady, and I was flattered, but I just wanted to be friends. Although I don't think I realized it at the time, I was saving my heart for Jack.

My life had become that of a typical American teenager growing up in Brooklyn in the 1950s. It was totally normal, maybe even a little predictable at times. It felt exactly as it was supposed to be.

I also found that when I wrote about my experiences in the Holocaust, the flashbacks and nightmares I still occasionally experienced got better. One day in high school, I wrote an essay about my experience as a hidden child. My English teacher told me it was very good and recommended to our school principal that it should be published in the yearbook. I was proud and excited and nervous, and glad that people would be able to learn about my story, as sad and difficult as it was.

But then I got called into the principal's office. I didn't know why. I'd always been a good student and well-behaved.

"Have a seat, Ruth," the principal said with a smile on his face. I saw he held my essay in his hand. "This is a very well-written story," he told me. "But I'm afraid it's too sad for our children. We won't be able to publish it in the yearbook."

I was stunned. Too sad for *our* children? Wasn't I a part of the student body too? And what about my classmates who had also lived through the Holocaust? I had hoped that even though my story might be upsetting at times, it ultimately would send an important message about tolerance and hope.

But the principal had made his message clear. It seemed the world wasn't quite ready to talk about the Holocaust yet. I hoped one day it would be.

24

Graduation, and Beyond

RIGHT BEFORE THE FIRST day of senior year, my friends and I went to pick up our senior pins. They had the school's initials and colors, and were no bigger than a thumbnail, but getting one was a *big* deal. We wore them on the right side of our sweaters every day until graduation.

On graduation day, the tradition was that the girls attached the pins to their gowns and the boys pinned them to the tassels on their caps.

Before I knew it, my own graduation day had

arrived. The year was 1951. The principal called my name—"Ruth Gamzer"—and I walked onstage to get my diploma. After filing back to my seat, I sat down and held my diploma with both hands. I thought back to when I got my visa and how important that piece of paper was to me. Now I had this.

I felt like I had the whole world ahead of me. Never did I think that I would be able to graduate on time. I had a piano at home and continued to play music, and I was in the school orchestra and part of an accordion band. I never thought I would make such close friends and keep in touch with many of them for the rest of my life. Before I met them, I had still felt alone in America. I hadn't known anyone else who started a new life as a teenage immigrant living in Brooklyn. Our common experience bound us together, and always would.

After graduating high school, I attended Brooklyn College. Right around that time was when I had my first encounter with anti-Semitism in America.

In addition to being a student, I also got a job working at an insurance company in Manhattan. Everyone at the office seemed friendly, especially a young woman who also came from Poland. One day, on a company excursion, this woman and I sat next to each other on the bus and began talking. She told me about herself, and I told her my whole story: how I was Jewish and had survived the Holocaust—everything.

The next morning, I was working at my desk when my supervisor came over to speak to me. It shocked me when he said, "You're a very nice girl, but you're not for us." I was being fired? Why? But somehow I understood—my coworker, whom I'd confided in, must have told the supervisor that I was Jewish. I was startled to learn that the hatred I'd known so well in Europe existed here too. Speechless, I gathered my things, got to my feet, and left.

I still needed to work, so I found a new job, also at an insurance company. My coworkers seemed friendly, but one day, while eating lunch, one of them said to me, "You're not Jewish, are you, Ruth?" I froze, too shocked to answer. A few weeks later, the Jewish holiday of Passover began. Passover, which falls during the springtime, commemorates when the Jewish people were freed from bondage in Egypt. During Passover, Jews eat a special unleavened bread called matzoh. I was afraid that if I brought my lunch—which contained matzoh—my coworkers would notice and see that I was indeed Jewish. The old fear rose up in me, and I quit that job immediately.

For my third job, I made a decision. I didn't want to hide anymore. I showed up to the job interview wearing a silver necklace with a Star of David pendant, proudly showing to the world that yes, I was Jewish. To my surprise, I was hired on the spot, and there were no issues at this new job.

Before I started my second year of college, Jack

moved to New York. He had been living in Detroit after finishing his service in the Korean War. Not long after he arrived, Jack took me out one night to see a movie. He was walking me home when he stopped and asked me to marry him—for real.

The word popped out of my mouth before I could even think it. "Yes!" I said. It was as if it had been meant to be, all along.

Jack and I got married right after my nineteenth birthday. We made our first home together near my parents in Brooklyn, and we went on to have two sons—first-generation Americans.

Epilogue: My Destiny

I HAD BEEN LIVING in Brooklyn for many years, married with children, when I started thinking about going back to Lvov. It is now called Lviv and is part of Ukraine. My mother told me not to go. She said it would be too sad, too painful to relive, too devastating. That I would suffer.

But I didn't listen. Something in me felt that I *had* to go back. I had to see what it was like now, after so long. The last time I was there felt like a lifetime ago. It seemed as if my memories of Lvov belonged to another person. Someone who never left Poland, or traveled by train from city to city all over Europe, or boarded a ship that crossed the Atlantic Ocean bound for America.

This time I took a plane across the Atlantic Ocean, with Jack at my side. When we arrived in Lviv, the city was familiar and also completely strange to me. There were pretty three-story town houses sandwiched together, with wrought-iron balconies and entrances at the sidewalk. Bustling Rynek Głowny—the main square—sat in the center of the old town, with a leafy park in the middle and a trolley traversing one end. The magnificent gilded opera house and spired churches looked like something from a fairy tale.

I wanted to see my old apartment, particularly the bathroom that had been my hiding spot with Henio, where we had held our breaths as Nazi boots thudded back and forth across the wood floor. Finding the building wasn't easy because the street names had changed several times in post-war years. After hours of wandering, Jack and I turned down a street that I vaguely recognized. Then there it was: number 18.

We walked up to the top floor, and when I finally gathered my nerves, I knocked on the door. A nice-looking middle-aged man answered. I explained to him that I had lived in the house with my parents before the war and asked if it would be okay if I looked around. I didn't tell him Jack and I were Jewish. I was still cautious about sharing that information. His wife was out, he told me, and then invited us inside.

A little girl who was about the age I had been when the war started was playing with a doll on the living room floor. I walked down the hall, through the rooms, and into the kitchen. When I reached the bathroom and put my hand on the doorknob, my legs suddenly felt as if they were going to buckle beneath me. I couldn't stop myself from crying.

"I have to go," I told Jack.

I turned and hurried away with my heart racing, handing the girl some money and muttering a thank-you to her father on the way. I flew down the steps gasping for breath and thought I was going to pass out until we got to the street.

My mother had been right. Going back was too difficult. I had imagined that Lviv would feel like home. Part of me wished it had, because I did have many happy memories of my early childhood. But it wasn't home anymore. Home was Brooklyn, where I had built my life and raised my family. When my flight back from Europe hit the runway in New York, I felt even more thankful than I was that day back in 1949, when I stepped off the *Marine Flasher* in Boston. I was reminded that here, in America, I had begun a new life.

❧

People often ask me at what point I felt I had become an American. Was it my first Independence Day celebration? When I spoke English without thinking about it? Or maybe it happened when I showed up at school wearing two different color socks. Perhaps it was when I got my citizenship, or when I returned to America from my visit to Lviv and felt so much relief.

Looking back, becoming American wasn't a single moment but rather a collection of smaller moments. It was something that built slowly over time.

Being American meant assimilating. It's easier to notice what's being lost rather than gained. I don't know that I ever felt more American, only less European. We were told to forget about our past and whatever horrible things we experienced during the Holocaust and start fresh. And that's what many of us wanted in the years after we emigrated. We didn't want to remember. Also, many Americans, like my high school principal, weren't ready to hear what we had to say.

But our silence was dangerous. People told our stories for us. If we had told them too, there would have been that many more voices speaking truth and, perhaps, that many more heard.

That is why, today, I feel it is so important to share my story, to remind people what hate and intolerance can do, and also what bravery and compassion can do as well. Just as I can never forget the atrocities of the Holocaust, I will never forget the incredible strength and generosity of my neighbors who risked their own lives to hide me and my parents. You never know how one act of kindness can change someone's life forever.

I knew I wanted to share my message with people. Jack and I were semi-retired and very happy as grandparents of four beautiful grandchildren, when I decided to take a course in public speaking through an organization called the Hidden Child Foundation. After graduating from the course, I became a gallery educator at the Museum of Jewish Heritage: A Living Memorial to the Holocaust and began giving tours at the museum. In fact, I even donated to the museum the dyed-blue pair of socks that I had worn while I was in hiding at the Oyaks', and the socks are still on display there today.

I had always loved to write but hadn't ever sat down to write my whole story. One day, a woman named Mara Bovsun interviewed me and Jack for a book she and another author named Allan Zullo were writing called *Survivors: True Stories of Children in the Holocaust*. The book featured my story, as well as Jack's. Mara encouraged me to write myself, so I took her writing course at New York University. Then I wrote my first memoir, *Destined to Live*, which was published in 2007. A novel based on Jack's life story, *Prisoner B-3087*, written by Alan Gratz, was published in 2013.

Jack and I began receiving invitations to schools all around the country, from Alabama to Arizona, to speak to students about our experiences during the Holocaust. Unfortunately, to this day, there are some people who believe the Holocaust never happened, that it was all a hoax; but Jack and I were living proof of that horrible time. We started receiving thousands of letters from students who, because of our stories, became interested in learning about the Holocaust, and history.

Sadly, Jack passed away in 2017, and I miss him every single day. Jack is missed by everyone who knew him. There are also so many people who never met Jack but have read about his story and feel touched and inspired by him.

Even though I've had aches and pains, and some problems with my health, somehow, miraculously, I've recovered each time. It often seems as if someone is watching over me. I've still felt strong enough to keep traveling and to keep speaking to young people about my experiences. I like to believe that we all have a specific destiny. And I often think it is my destiny to share these messages of peace and tolerance, especially when so much prejudice, hate, and racism still exist in the world.

I tell young people that just as the world is beautiful because of the variety in nature—like different types of flowers coming together to make a bouquet—so too are humans beautiful because of our differences. And also, our similarities. I believe that regardless of our backgrounds or the color of our skin, we all share the same humanity, and we are deserving of empathy. Today, people from all over the world are being forced to leave their homes because of their ethnicity, race, or religion. In a way, their struggles are similar to the struggles I experienced as a displaced person in Europe. Our stories are not so different. There is more that unites us than divides us. If there is any message I'd like to pass along, it's that.

A Special Note from Ruth Gruener

Dear Readers,

I want to thank you very much for reading about my life.

I was once told that a blessing from a survivor comes true.

So, I want to wish every one of you the best of health and a long life in a peaceful world.

Love,

Ruth Gruener

Ruth at age two, in Poland. This photograph was the one hanging on the wall the day the Nazi soldier came to Ruth's house while she hid in the bathroom and narrowly escaped capture.

Ruth at age four with her parents, Barbara and Isaac Gamzer, in Poland. Ruth, an only child, was extremely close to her parents and was devastated to be separated from them when she first went into hiding.

Ruth and her kindergarten class in Poland before the war. Ruth is the fifth girl from the right in the back row. Ruth is the only child in this whole class who survived the Holocaust; every other student was killed.

These are the socks Ruth wore when she was in hiding. She donated them to the Museum of Jewish Heritage: A Living Memorial to the Holocaust in New York City.

Ruth after the war, as an almost-teenager living in Munich, Germany.

Moje Zwierciadełko

Monachium 8 VI 1947 r.

The front page of Ruth's diary, which she got while living in Munich. The words "My Little Mirror" are written here in Polish, along with the location and date: "Munich, June 8, 1947."

The SS *Marine Flasher* was the ship Ruth and her parents took to come to America in 1949. This is a photograph of that same ship arriving in New York Harbor in 1946. The *Marine Flasher* was a former troop transport ship that was used to bring displaced persons like Ruth and her parents from Europe to the United States.

Ruth (in the center) poses with her friends from James Madison High School in Brooklyn, New York, while other classmates look on. It was difficult to adjust to life in America, but Ruth was grateful to find new friends in school.

Ruth's high school graduation photograph. Ruth was very proud to graduate from Thomas Jefferson High School in Brooklyn, New York.

A photograph of Jack Gruener, Ruth's future husband, as a young US soldier. After surviving ten concentration camps during the Holocaust, Jack immigrated to America, where he was drafted into the army to fight in the Korean War. Ruth wrote him letters while he was overseas.

Ruth and Jack on their wedding day, in Brooklyn, New York. They built a happy life together and went on to have two sons and four grandchildren.

In 2005, Ruth (on the right) was reunited with Joanna Zalucka (Jasia Szczygiel) when Joanna came to visit the United States. They had not seen each other since 1944, and it was an emotional moment, full of tears and gratitude. Their reunion was documented by the local news.

Ruth Gruener was born Aurelia Gamser in 1930s Poland. Ruth and her parents survived the Holocaust, and immigrated to the United States after the war. Ruth married Jack Gruener, another Holocaust survivor, whose true story inspired the book *Prisoner B-3087*. Ruth lives in Brooklyn, New York, and works as a docent at the Museum of Jewish Heritage in Manhattan. She travels all over the country to speak to schools about her experiences during the Holocaust.

Alan Gratz is the New York Times bestselling author of several award-winning and acclaimed books for young readers, including *Prisoner B-3087* and *Refugee*. Alan lives in North Carolina with his wife and daughter. Look for him online at alangratz.com.